The Main course

Front cover and inside photography: James Jackson
Stylist: Jackie Jackson
Home economist: Alyson Birch
Back cover photograph: Natalie Legg

Line illustrations: Tony Spaul

Published by BBC Books,
A division of BBC Enterprises Ltd
Woodlands, 80 Wood Lane, London W12 0TT

First published 1989
© The author 1989

ISBN 0 563 21468 6

Typeset in 11/12 Baskerville
by Phoenix Photosetting, Chatham
Colour separations by Technik Ltd, Berkhamsted

Printed and bound in Great Britain by
Mackays of Chatham PLC, Chatham, Kent

Cover printed by Richard Clay Ltd, Norwich

The Main course

Susan Hicks

BBC Books

Acknowledgements

So many people have inspired and helped me with *The Main Course*, and I thank them all. In particular, I must say thank you to my sister Diana for lending me her flat in Lincoln, where for a few weeks I was a regular customer of Mr Larry Dickens (licensed game dealer and quality butcher of Bailgate in the shadow of Lincoln Cathedral), who gave me much advice on the subject of game. I would also like to thank Mr Ian Lentern, quality butcher of Penzance who raises his own animals which he sells in his shop in Chapel Street, and who is of the opinion that we must return to our native breeds, and correct feeding in non-intensive systems for the improvement of our beef and other meat. Special thanks are due to Daphne MacCarthy from the British Food Information Service of Food from Britain from whose invaluable publication *Prodfact* I drew much information for the chapters on meat production and types of cuts available. The Meat and Livestock Commission supplied reams of informative leaflets, as did the British Egg and the British Chicken Information Service. Many individual food producers, too numerous to mention, were helpful and happy to talk with enthusiasm, and in particular I would like to thank Anne Petch of Heal Farm and Richard Guy of The Real Meat Company – two champions of quality additive-free meat. The Soil Association pointed me in the direction of the growing number of organic producers of vegetables, eggs and meat, and information from Compassion in World Farming served to heighten my awareness of the perils of inhumane methods of meat production.

Love and thanks to all my family and friends who gather around my table at Blue Barn on the island; to Rhondda Wraithe of Gugh Island who kindly tested several of the recipes, and to Natalie Legg for taking my photograph for the book at the quay where her husband lands his daily catch of lobsters and crabs.

During the twenty or so years that I have been cooking at our island home, overlapping recipes and ideas have been absorbed from many sources, and in 'further reading' at the end of this book, I do include my favourite cookery writers to whom I am deeply indebted.

Susan Hicks
July 1989

Contents

Conversion Table

All these are approximate conversions, which have either been rounded up or down. In a few recipes it has been necessary to modify them very slightly. Never mix metric and imperial measures in one recipe. Stick to one system or the other.

Weights

½ oz	10 g
1	25
1½	40
2	50
3	75
4	110
5	150
6	175
7	200
8	225
9	250
10	275
12	350
13	375
14	400
15	425
1 lb	450
1¼	550
1½	700
2	900
3	1.4 kg
4	1.8
5	2.3

Volume

1 fl oz	25 ml
2	50
3	75
5 (¼ pint)	150
10 (½)	300
15 (¾)	400
1 pint	570
1¼	700
1½	900
1¾	1 litre
2	1.1
2¼	1.3
2½	1.4
2¾	1.6
3	1.7
3¼	1.8
3½	2
3¾	2.1
4	2.3
5	2.8
6	3.4
7	4.0
8 (1 gal)	4.5

Measurements

¼ inch	0.5 cm
½	1
1	2.5
2	5
3	7.5
4	10
6	15
7	18
8	20.5
9	23
11	28
12	30.5

Oven temperatures

Mk 1	275°F	140°C
2	300	150
3	325	170
4	350	180
5	375	190
6	400	200
7	425	220
8	450	230
9	475	240

Imperial spoon measures are used throughout the book. These are *level* spoonfuls. If you have a set of metric spoons, use the following equivalents: 1 teaspoon = 5 ml; 1 tablespoon = 15 ml.

Introduction

Who would have thought, a decade or two ago, that supermarkets and food shops would carry such a fascinating and diverse range of ingredients as many of them do today? Over the years, television food and cookery programmes and hundreds of cook books and magazines have stimulated a huge and growing enthusiasm for cooking – Chinese-, Indian- and Mediterranean-style; organic, vegetarian, fish and game cookery; cooking healthily, fussily, scientifically or simply; cooking by microwave, steamer, barbecue, fan-assisted oven or halogen hob. Even so, it is hardly surprising that there is much muddled thinking about food and cooking. What a mish-mash of conflicting advice on nutrition and diet we have been fed! Deep into our psyche floods all the information and mis-information, often resulting in extremes of eating behaviour and guilt-ridden closet eating of 'undesirable' food. And as for those gleaming battalions of shiny fruits and vegetables – many of them out-of-season and cottonwool-textured – and ranks of cling-wrapped indefinable meats: just what are we to make of their uniform blandness?

At last a clear message seems to be coming through. A renewed interest has arisen in the quality and freshness of seasonal 'real' food – pure and simple; a renaissance which takes heed of sensible moderation and steers a main course towards what is reasonable, practical and enjoyable. Today there is a growing army of regional food producers in this country who can scarcely keep up with the demand for their speciality foods – wonderful traditional cheeses, organically grown vegetables, meat and game, oysters, smoked fish – and a growing public who are discovering, or rediscovering, the flavour of food as it was before the crazy era of intensive farming, food processing and fast profits.

Few people can claim to be totally disinterested in the occasion of eating, even if they are not so keen on cooking. And the food we eat, and the table we keep, is like a secret language. It can reflect snobbishness, competitiveness or one-upmanship. It can convey warmth, sheer wizardry and simple pleasure. An apparently unassuming table can breathe of the pleasant hour or so in which you might have podded some fresh young peas, scrubbed the first bundle of carrots or ground up a little delight of spices or herbs – all the magic and individual touches that transform the simplest of ingredients and bring sheer joy to the table.

There isn't much excuse for claiming that your local shops cannot or will not stock good-quality local produce. *You* must create the demand. Even my own local island post office and store has changed – slowly but dramatically – from stocking basic carrots, onions, apples and oranges with a conservative range of tinned provisions. Now it offers an intelligently chosen range of fresh vegetables (locally grown where possible) and superb fruit. Good pasta, basmati rice, herbs, pulses, poppadums and dried fruits mingle with favourite staples like tinned sardines, kidney beans, tuna and baked beans. As all good shopkeepers should be, our postmistress is ever willing to order the unusual or the difficult-to-obtain. And this on a remote island with a population of sixty!

I don't think that there can be much excuse either for saying that you do not have time to do 'proper' cooking. A speedily made dish of fresh pasta tossed with olive oil, garlic, herbs and a few lightly cooked mushrooms, sprinkled with a grating of gorgeous Cheddar cheese or fresh Parmesan and served with a crisp green salad, is infinitely preferable to most convenience foods. You can easily prepare this during the time a gluey bland frozen lasagne takes to cook.

In *The Main Course* I have endeavoured to show that good food need not be expensive, time-consuming or difficult to cook. I very much hope that you will find – as in my earlier book, *The Fish Course* – that the simplest food, simply prepared with no fuss, is the best in the world.

The subject of healthy eating and nutrition is highly intricate. However, we love and crave certain foods mainly because of early conditioning: hence an occasional incomprehensible desire for steak and kidney pie after your hundredth Greek salad while swatting off the mosquitoes in a heatwave, or a strange longing for mushy peas and boiled ham in a sacred Indian temple.

Therefore I have not neglected our favourite roasts, stews and pies – traditional British food which need not be stodgy or fatty when cooked with care. And in reflecting the cosmopolitan influence on our daily main course, I have also included many recipes from around the world. On the whole, I think this collection epitomises our concern for wholesome healthy eating and happy moderation. I hope you will have the greatest pleasure in cooking and adapting the recipes – while using the very best, very freshest, seasonal ingredients.

The bad news – intensive food production

The year 1989, in which I write this, is Food and Farming Year and never a more opportune time to examine our attitudes to the production methods in the food and farming industries. In a year when a wealthy 'civilised' Western country should be celebrating its designated food year in clear conscience that its produce is blameless, wholesome, healthy, nutritious and humanely produced, it is ironic that a surge of panics and scandals about that produce should hit the headlines; ironic and most timely.

I am dismayed that, time and again, we show concern or outrage about such scandals only as far as our own personal health and lifestyle are concerned. (The general reaction to the discovery of salmonella in eggs and chickens is an obvious recent and notorious example.) We demand cheap and plentiful food and we take food from the shelves of our shops with no natural curiosity about or regard for how it has been reared, slaughtered, harvested or manufactured.

We are well known as a nation of animal lovers, given to a degree of sentimentality and love for our pets that quite perplexes the inhabitants of other countries. But something in our national character seems to switch off and turn away from the cruelty inflicted on animals that feel fear and pain in just the same way as our pampered cats, dogs and other favourite pets. The unhappy life and squalid death of one intensively reared, carelessly slaughtered and subsequently frozen chicken is hardly likely to be a priority in our thoughts as we do our shopping – any more than the close confinement of pregnant sows in dry stalls (where they cannot even turn around, let alone root and forage) and countless other inhumane and intensive methods of rearing livestock. But we should remember that, apart from tacitly allowing the suffering inflicted on these animals, we are at the end of a chain of synthetic animal-growth promoters, artificial hormones, antibiotics and various chemicals (given to them in both food and medication) whose long-term effects on our own health are unknown.

Nor do we always pause to think of the harm we are doing to ourselves and our land when we buy vegetables produced with the rampant use of herbicides, pesticides and chemical fertilisers.

It is becoming clear that whether or not we really care about our environment and a holistic and harmonious approach to food production, too high a proportion of the food we eat leaves much to be desired. Food-related disease, allergies, illness and even deaths have been linked to some processed, refined and manufactured foods – and now an accusing finger is being pointed at intensive farming.

The good news – 'real food' revival

'It's not easy being green,' sings my favourite frog, Kermit, in his famous tragic lament – but millions disagree. It is very heartening to see all manner of green consumerism responding to pioneering farmers and food producers who in turn are striving through the first difficult production years of establishing organic crops and organic pasture for animals reared in natural (or at least 'high welfare') conditions. Also encouraging for genuine lovers of 'real' food is the renewed enthusiasm for traditional breeds of livestock – and here it should be mentioned that this is not a yuppie revival. There are many farmers of the old school who have stubbornly refused against the odds to bow to fashion. Likewise there are many traditional butchers, game dealers and fishmongers who remain steadfast and faithful to their craft, give exemplary service and – in my experience in researching *The Main Course* – despair of the many government agencies and business conglomerates which conspire to persuade them to offer inferior quality in order that they and the food producers and farmers may enjoy greater short-term profits.

The Main Course is a recipe book which includes a brief introductory guide to wholesome, free-range ingredients and basic techniques. It does not set out to be an encyclopaedia or bible, but I hope it reflects an embracing joy in food, company, eating and in the atmosphere and environment in which the ingredients are produced. I am a cook who, in common with many others, is neither a 'bunny hugger', nor a sentimental vegetarian, nor an uncaring and ruthless carnivore. The books and organisations mentioned in Further Reading on page 218 will be of interest to you if you wish to make intelligent enquiry into 'alternative' methods of food production. It is good to know that, in shopping with consideration of the source of our food, we will be rewarded not only by its being of better quality and flavour but also by each extra penny we pay subscribing to a return to natural farming methods and to a rescue of our ravaged environment.

Susan Hicks
June 1989

Ingredients

One of the most pleasurable ingredients in cooking and eating is *anticipation*. And for me this is nearly always inspired by what is seasonal, fresh and – whenever possible – locally produced. I love the first picking or cutting, the first lifting or podding . . . tiny new potatoes, sweet crunchy carrots, spring lamb, wild mint . . . and we are just beginning to appreciate again the huge diversity of wonderful vegetables, cheeses and speciality foods that are produced throughout the regions of Britain. Of course, this produce jostles along with welcome partners of similar foods from Europe and further afield.

The store-cupboard

The store-cupboard is an extremely important auxiliary to fresh ingredients. As I live on an island, I am cursed with a siege mentality and am panic-stricken when I visit mainland friends with sparse food cupboards and bare refrigerators. With the provisions I keep, it has been suggested that I could open a small shop, or at least eat splendidly for months without spending another penny! If you are busy and prone to buying convenience foods or take-aways, you might be surprised to find how easy, satisfyingly creative and cheap it is to conjure up supper without a dash to the late-night supermarket. Dried, tinned and bottled standbys, such as oils, vinegars, herbs, spices, rice, pulses and pasta, olives, vine leaves, sardines, tomatoes, a range of flours and cereals and dried fruits, mustards, crispbreads and biscuits and so on are all waiting there – like an artist's palate.

The freezer

The space available in the average domestic fridge/freezer is somewhat limited for ambitious freezing of garden surplus, whole sides of lamb and so on, but is ideal for one of my essential ingredients – home-made stock. Prepared in quantity and frozen in small amounts (see page 12), simple vegetable, chicken, game and fish stocks are there at hand when you do not have the time or patience to make them from scratch. They add quality, body and flavour to all manner of soups, sauces and casseroles. And combined with rice or pasta from your store-cupboard they can provide the basis of instant and effortless meals.

Another advantage of having a freezer for the one- or two-person household is that you can freeze the remaining half of a dish that is difficult to cook in small amounts – a casserole, say, or a savoury flan, gratin or risotto. These can be life-savers when you are too busy or tired to prepare a meal and are infinitely preferable to frozen convenience food.

See page 20 for information on freezing and thawing meat.

Stocks

Home-made stock is an essential ingredient of good cooking, and may be as simple or as complicated as you wish. Good home-made gravies and sauces enhance and transform the simplest of offerings. Highly seasoned instant sauces produced from packets, tins or cubes dominate and kill the subtle flavours of freshly cooked food.

Not many modern kitchens and lifestyles can support the running of an old-fashioned everlasting stockpot. And in these days of heightened concern about careful food preparation, it is particularly appreciated that stocks should be freshly made, cooled, skimmed and either stored in the refrigerator in readiness for a specific recipe or frozen in small tubs or ice-cube trays. Cubes of concentrated (reduced) stocks are invaluable when 1 or 2 tablespoons of essence are required for a sauce. Once the cubes have frozen in the tray, tap them out and transfer them to small polythene freezer bags (they will not stick together), label them and use as required. They will keep in the freezer for up to 6 months.

Generally, stocks for the family kitchen can be made up from cooked or uncooked carcasses and trimmings; bones from a joint; fish bones, head and trimmings; the shells and heads of shellfish; miscellaneous vegetables (preferably not from the strong-tasting cabbage family); peelings from scrubbed vegetables; mushroom stalks; squashy tomatoes; outer stems from celery; and herbs. You can also add left-over gravy and white or red wine. With regard to the ingredients that go into these sorts of individual stocks from the kitchen, this is a matter of preference and common sense. Very pungent herbs will overwhelm and too much salt and other seasonings may become too concentrated if the stock is reduced.

Long slow cooking (3–4 hours) on top of the stove or in a low oven is the general rule for preparing home-made stocks – except for fish stock which rarely takes more than 30 minutes. After 3 or 4 hours of low simmering, the stock should be strained, cooled and then refrigerated for a few hours until it is possible to remove any solidified fat from the surface. To speed up this process, pour the strained stock into a chilled bowl (which could, if you wish, be sitting in a larger bowl of ice cubes), and drop an ice cube or two into the stock itself to cool it rapidly and force the fat to the top.

Stocks need not be a huge effort if you can fit their making into the day-to-day rhythm of the kitchen, and once you have stored or frozen them you have the most magical ingredient to hand at a moment's notice.

Some of *The Main Course* recipes give individual instructions for stock making, as for example in the case of game. The following are useful basic stocks:

Brown stock

The best stocks come from raw bones (usually beef or veal) which are first browned to give colour and flavour. Although the cooking time is long and slow, the preparation is relatively simple and certainly worthwhile. Once strained, the finished stock may be boiled down to reduce and concentrate it, and then stored in the refrigerator or frozen. The basic flavouring vegetables may be varied somewhat, but bear in mind that potatoes will produce a cloudy stock, and some root vegetables have a strong and dominant taste. It is not advisable to add salt at the beginning as the stock will become too concentrated if it is to be reduced. If you want a gelatinous stock, add a pig's trotter.

A simpler beef stock may be produced from the ingredients listed below by leaving out the initial roasting stage, but the flavour will not be so full. The simmering process may be speeded up by using a pressure-cooker, cooking for 50 minutes with a 15 lb (6.75 kg) weight.

The quantities in the following recipe may be adjusted to taste.

2½–3½ lb (1.25–1.65 kg) beef bones, chopped into small pieces

2 onions, peeled and chopped

2 large carrots, chopped

1–2 sticks celery, sliced

1–2 cloves garlic, halved

Parsley stalks, broken

6–8 peppercorns

1 posy fresh herbs

Optional extras:

1 rasher streaky bacon, diced

Scraps of fresh raw meat

Brown onion skins

Mushroom stalks or *porcini* (ceps)

1–2 tomatoes, chopped

Juniper berries

1 bay leaf

1 blade mace

Pre-heat the oven to gas mark 7, 425°F (220°C).

Arrange the bones in a layer on the base of a large roasting tin and roast in the oven for 40 minutes, turning them occasionally. Take care not to let them burn or become dark brown, or the stock will be bitter: aim for an even golden-brown colour.

Transfer the bones to a very large pan. Put the roasting tin over a medium heat and gently fry the vegetables in the fat that has run out of the bones until they are also golden-brown. At this stage, if there is not enough fat, you could first fry the diced bacon (if using) in the tin until the fat runs, and then add the vegetables. Tip the vegetables and bacon (if using) into the pan of bones and cover with water; you will probably need about 4 pints (2.25 litres). Bring *slowly and gently* to the boil, then immediately turn down the heat to barely simmering and skim off the scum. Never allow the stock to boil rapidly or the fat will emulsify. Now add the parsley stalks, peppercorns, herbs and scraps of meat (if using). Cover with a lid, but leave a small gap for the steam to escape. Cook very gently on top of the stove for at least 4 hours or until you feel you have obtained as much flavour as possible. From time to time skim off any scum that collects on the surface and, if necessary, top up with more *boiling* water to keep the bones covered. Strain into a clean pan or bowl, cool, refrigerate, remove the fat, and store or use as required.

Basic fish stock

Use the head, tail and bones of fish to make a good basic stock. Your fishmonger will give or sell you 'frames', which are the whole fish minus the fillets. Oily fish such as mackerel and herring are not suitable for stock making. If you happen to have them, add the shells of prawns or crab for an extra-tasty stock.

Makes about 2 pints (1·1 litres)

1½ lb (700 g) fish trimmings (head, bones, skin, scraps)

1½ pints (900 ml) water

1 onion, peeled and sliced

1 carrot, chopped

1 leek, chopped

10 fl oz (300 ml) white wine or cider

Pinch of salt

Broken parsley stalks or bouquet garni

6 black peppercorns, crushed or bruised

Put everything except the peppercorns into a large saucepan, bring to the boil and simmer for no more than 30 minutes, skimming from time to time. Add the peppercorns for the last 10 minutes of cooking time.

Chicken stock

Chicken stock may be produced from uncooked or cooked carcasses, chicken pieces or trimmings (though it is advisable not to mix raw and cooked bones) with the addition of the giblets. For a very plain light chicken stock, place the carcass and meat scraps in a large pan, cover well with water, season lightly and bring to the boil. Skim off the scum that rises to the surface, lower the heat and barely simmer for about 3 hours. Strain into a clean bowl, cool, skim and blot off the fat, and store or use as required.

For extra flavour, add the following after bringing to the boil and skimming off the scum:

2 onions, quartered but unpeeled

2–3 sticks celery, chopped

2 carrots, chopped

A few black peppercorns

1 posy fresh herbs

Milk, lemon and herb stock

This stock, which needs no preliminary cooking, is excellent for white fish and smoked fish such as haddock or cod. The acidity of the lemon heightens the flavour of the fish.

Makes 1 pint (570 ml)

10 fl oz (300 ml) full cream or semi-skimmed milk

10 fl oz (300 ml) water

2–3 lemons, peeled and sliced

Pinch of salt

Freshly ground black pepper

1 bouquet garni or crushed parsley stalks

Simply combine all the ingredients. To avoid curdling when poaching fish in this stock, it is more than usually important not to let it boil. Poach in the normal manner. The strained liquid can form the basis of many different creamy soups or sauces.

Thickening sauces with flour – roux and beurre manié

Flour-based sauces and gravies have lost favour in recent years, but when well made they taste delicious. They vary in consistency: a thinnish sauce is used to accompany food; a slightly thicker sauce to coat food and a still thicker sauce to bind.

To make a *roux*, use equal quantities – usually 1–2 oz (25–50 g) – fat (usually butter or dripping) and flour. Put the fat in a small heavy saucepan and heat gently until it melts. Take it off the heat, add the flour and stir well in to form a paste. Return to the heat and cook on for about 2 minutes. Take the pan off the heat again and add the warm liquid gradually, whisking to form a smooth mixture. Return to the heat again and cook for several minutes, stirring all the time, until the floury taste is cooked out and the desired thickness is achieved.

To make a *beurre manié*, fork together equal quantities of butter and flour – usually 1–2 oz (25–50 g) of each – until a smooth paste is achieved. Gradually add small scraps of this paste to the sauce or gravy. As they melt and incorporate into the liquid, the sauce will gradually thicken. Continue stirring and cooking for several minutes to cook out the floury taste.

A few notes on special ingredients used in this book

Chilli peppers
There are various types of these members of the capsicum or pepper family. They are available fresh or dried, red or green, large or small, and some are stronger than others. The seeds are particularly fiery and are often removed before the pepper is chopped and used in a recipe: simply split the pepper lengthways to de-seed. Care must be taken not to rub your eyes with your fingers after dealing with the seeds – either wear rubber gloves or wash your hands very thoroughly afterwards. However, the peppers may be sliced and used seeds and all if you want a very hot and spicy dish. It is best to be on the safe side and use chillies sparingly when trying them for the first time.

Filo (or strudel) pastry
Unlike conventional pastry ingredients, which generally require a cool temperature and a light touch, the warm ingredients of filo are beaten and kneaded in a complicated process to produce paper-thin sheets of 'pulled dough' pastry. Therefore it is fortunate that good filo pastry is available frozen in 1 lb (450 g) packets. Filo is used for Middle Eastern sweet and

savoury pastries, and is identical to the European strudel pastry. Each one of the required number of sheets is brushed with melted butter or oil and layered as directed in the recipe (for example, Minty Lamb in Filo Pastry, page 93; Celeriac, Pine Nut and Goat's Cheese Strudels, page 190), producing a similar result to puff pastry, but lighter and crispier. When using a batch of filo pastry, keep the pile from which you are working covered with a clean damp teatowel to prevent it becoming dry and brittle. The beauty of frozen filo is that the unused remaining sheets can be re-rolled, returned to their packet and re-frozen.

Lavabread

Lavabread is a species of seaweed. In Wales, where it is usually mixed with oatmeal, formed into small cakes and fried with bacon, it is a speciality. It makes a delicious sauce and is available in cans from delicatessens and good food halls. Simply heat through gently with a knob of butter and a squeeze of lemon or bitter orange juice. It is good with lamb (see page 88).

Lemon grass

Lemon grass is a fragrant yet quite potent grass. The tougher outer leaves may be used as flavouring, and the soft inner stalk sliced across like a spring onion and eaten raw or cooked. (See Salmon with Lemon Grass, page 184.)

Mussels

Always buy fresh live mussels from a reliable source. They should be tightly closed before cooking and open up when they are cooked. If they are gaping as you scrub them, give them a tap or two – they should clam up immediately; otherwise discard them (in the words of the late and great Peter Langhan, 'the buggers are dead!'). You should also throw away any that do not open up when cooked, or are cracked or damaged. Scrub each mussel thoroughly and pull away the beard – a stubborn hairy tuft. Scrape away any barnacles and other debris. To steam open mussels, put them in a large pan with a little liquid – water or wine – over a medium heat: you may have to do this in batches. As they open, which will take just a few minutes, use a perforated spoon to remove them for use as required and take care to keep their juices and strained cooking liquor.

Sausage casings

Natural casings (made from animal gut) may be available from your own butcher, or may be obtained by mail order from specialists. They are usually dried and salted, and will need soaking overnight before use. Pig's gut is the most usual for casing a standard-sized sausage and is the easiest to buy. Sheep's gut is used for chipolata-size and ox's for very large sausages such as *mortadella*. Caul, the lacy fat stomach lining of the pig, is used to wrap forcemeat mixtures like faggots – the fat bastes the meat as it cooks.

Beef, lamb and pork

Unless you are buying meat from a helpful, knowledgeable, quality butcher, you are unlikely to be able to learn the age of the meat at slaughter, the period of hanging, the method of farming and the type of feed on which the animal was reared. You might imagine such considerations to be purely academic, but these are the facts which will determine the taste, cookability and quality. Furthermore, you might wish to consider the benefits of humane farming methods, organic pastures and residue-free feedstuffs (see page 9).

It is impossible in this short chapter to examine the many intricacies of breeding and cross-breeding and the history and development of meat production, but happily there is a growing interest in and trend towards producing top-quality meat from English breeds, conservation-grade meat and meat reared without the use of antibiotics or other chemicals; and in free-range poultry and game. (See page 218 for Further Reading and addresses of suppliers.)

Shopping for meat

In general try to patronise butchers who clearly demonstrate their craft by displaying beautifully butchered and prepared joints and cuts, and who can tell you the sources of their various meats, offer advice on cooking and prepare meat to your requirements, however small the amount or inexpensive the cut. Such butchers may charge higher prices, but if you have ever bought a badly butchered frozen pork chop with a cardboard-like flavour, or indefinable 'stewing steak' that tastes like soggy skirting board, you will have come to the conclusion that it is well worth spending a little – or even quite a lot – more on your meat.

Traditional cuts, Continental cuts and fat

All meat is composed, in simple terms, of water, protein and fat. This fat is saturated, and saturated fat, be it in dairy products or meat, is the kind that we are advised to cut down on because of its association with cholesterol and heart disease. However, in the traditional British cuts – even today, when meat is generally reared to be leaner – there is a limit to the amount of visible fat that can be trimmed away because joints and cuts are usually cut across the muscle. One answer to this problem is the Continental style of cutting, which is entirely different. It involves the technique of seaming out individual muscles and removing all waste gristle and connective tissue, so producing very lean, compact, boneless cuts.

Yet whichever method of butchery is employed, many would argue that nowadays there is a lack of depth and roundness of flavour in joints and steaks, and in slow braises and stews, unless the cooking methods are modified. For example, smothering joints in various marinades or flavourings and wrapping them in foil to minimise their dryness is suggested by the proponents and marketers of leaner meat for health. But I do not think that marinating joints is a particularly effective method for tenderising or adding flavour. A marinade cannot penetrate the middle of the meat; and often it alters the texture of the outer edge of a joint. On the other hand, there are some advantages in marinating smaller less fatty cuts, especially for quick convenient dishes like stir-fries, grills and kebabs.

The truth is that fat plays a vital part in both the texture and flavour of meat during cooking. In his book, *The Science and Lore of the Kitchen*, Harold McGee explains: 'Fat contributes to the tenderness of meat by acting as a "shortening" agent, much as it does in pastry. When it is melted during cooking, fat penetrates the tissue and helps separate fibre from fibre, lubricating the tissue and so making it easier to cut across or crush. Without much fat, otherwise tender meat becomes dry and resistant.'

By now you will be throwing up your hands in horror – what of the effect of saturated fats upon your health? I do not believe that sacrificing the flavour of traditional, healthily reared meat (with some fat on it) by choosing leaner, probably intensively reared meat is justifiable. When you turn to the recipe section of this book, you will find that meat can be cooked with all the flavour and other attributes that fat imparts, and then finished by removing that fat to produce succulent well-flavoured meat with a clear fat-free sauce or gravy. You might also consider paying more for and eating less meat as well as cutting down on other 'cholesterol culprits' in your diet, such as eggs, butter, cheese and milk.

In short, intelligent moderation and sympathetic cooking is the answer.

Freezing and thawing meat

Freezing meat, which we think of as a modern method of preserving, is actually older than you might imagine, but large-scale commercial freezing didn't start until around 1880. In 1923 Clarence Birdseye was the first to exploit the method of rapid freezing which minimises damage in foods.

Freezing is such an extreme treatment that it is bound to have some effect on the texture of meat. But with careful thawing and tender loving cooking, the results can be quite acceptable. Many butchers and farmers rate frozen meat as second-class, but the freezer is often invaluable to the cook for practical and economical reasons and therefore cannot be entirely dismissed. The freezing process inevitably results in 'drip': the loss of fluid rich in valuable proteins, vitamins and salts when the meat is thawed. Because of this loss of fluid, the meat, when cooked, may be tougher and dryer than fresh meat.

To maintain the quality in frozen meat stored over long periods, a low temperature is essential. This must certainly not be higher than 0°F (-18°C), the normal running temperature of the domestic freezer. The meat should be tightly wrapped in airtight, waterproof material both to prevent the surface drying out and to avoid cross-contamination of flavours within the freezer. For the latter reason you should also keep different types of food (meat, fish, cakes, pastries and so on) in separate compartments or trays in the freezer.

Because the fat in beef is mostly saturated and relatively stable, it can be frozen for much longer periods than lamb, pork, poultry and offal. The following storage times for various types of meat are recommended:

Joints of beef	Use within 12 months
Joints of lamb	Use within 9 months
Joints of pork	Use within 6 months
Minced meat	Use within 3 months
Bacon joints (vacuum-packed)	Use within 3 months
Bacon rashers	Use within 1 month
Bacon rashers (vacuum-packed)	Use within 3 months
Sausages	Use within 3 months

It is inadvisable to freeze salted meat – cured or pickled – because its storage life is unpredictable and generally very short. Bacon, unless vacuum-packed, has a very short storage life as salt accelerates rancidity.

The following storage times for cooked dishes are recommended:

Casseroles with bacon	3 months
Casseroles without bacon	6 months
Curried dishes	4 months
Meat pies	3 months
Pâté	1 month
Sliced meat with gravy	3 months
Sliced meat without gravy	6 months
Shepherd's pie	3 months
Soups	3 months

If you use your freezer constantly, it really is important to label each pack of food with full details of its contents and the date of freezing. You should also employ a good rotation system. If, like me, you are absent-minded and only occasionally use your freezer for meat, it is even more vital not to trust to memory. A survey of my labels reveals the following sample: 'Beef from Galloway trip, date . . ., but eat soon', or 'Harry's home-made sausages, date . . .', or 'Fabulous casserole, Ben's birthday, incl. garlic, bacon, super sauce etc., date . . .'. This kind of information brings vividly to mind just what delights are to be re-lived and which otherwise might not be identified simply by staring at mysterious food packages frozen months previously.

When it comes to thawing joints of meat, I have seen awful things done in home kitchens: the joint soaked in hot water or left on the back of a warm stove or even cooked from frozen (risky unless you have a meat thermometer, and it does not give good results). Meat should ideally be thawed slowly in the refrigerator, unwrapped then covered, which may take up to two days. Otherwise, thawing at room temperature or in the microwave is fine as long as you intend to cook the meat straight away by introducing it to a high temperature. Just think of all the bacteria present in meat: they love a warm atmosphere and increase a thousandfold or more in such conditions as every hour passes.

Chops and steaks obviously thaw more quickly than joints, but the same principles apply. Remember to wrap chops individually when freezing so that they can be separated easily and used as required.

Cuts and cooking methods

Beef

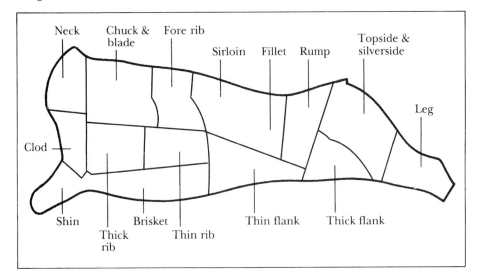

There are many types of beef cattle, and they are not all reared in the same way. Some are reared completely on one farm, carefully fed on concentrates and grass products. Intensively reared beef cattle are housed throughout their life and fed on an all-concentrate diet, then slaughtered at 10–12 months of age. Others are kept on grass/cereal systems in which the cattle are either winter-fed on conserved grass supplemented with concentrates, or grass-finished at 20–24 months old. There are large differences in growth rate between breeds which lead to substantial differences in the weights of carcass produced. Most of the well-established British beef breeds, such as the Aberdeen Angus and Hereford, are ready for slaughter at a relatively early age. At the other extreme, many of the Continental European breeds, such as the Charolais and Simmental, are very lean and have a late finishing age.

It used to be thought that deep-coloured meat was well-hung and would therefore be tender; and that paler meat was not properly hung and would therefore be tough. But the quality and appearance of beef is dependent on age, breed, feed and the sex of the animal, and on the hanging, storing and cutting up of the carcass. The colour of the meat does not indicate the eating quality, nor does the colour of the fat. The former is bright red when first cut but darkens quite quickly to become much browner. Again, the fat depends on the breed, age and sex of the animal and can be affected by the way the animal is fed.

In general, beef should look fresh and moist – not watery and limp – with small flecks of fat (marbling) through the lean.

For pedigree, pure-bred and conservation beef, reared in non-intensive systems and avoiding potentially harmful additives and artificial treatments, seek out the specialist retailers and farmers who are members of the Guild of Conservation (or see page 218 for Further Reading and addresses).

The cuts are as follows:

Shin (fore leg) and leg (hind leg) Lean meat but with a high proportion of connective tissue. Suitable for stews, casseroles, stock, soup, brawn.

Neck and clod Usually cut into pieces and sold as stewing steak or mince.

Chuck and blade steak Large, fairly lean cut of high quality. When removed from the bone, it is sold as 'chuck steak'. Suitable for braising, stewing, pie fillings.

Thick flank (top rump) A lean cut suitable for roasting, pot-roasting, braising or, when thinly sliced, for frying.

Thin flank Suitable for braising or stewing. Can be salted or pickled. Frequently sold minced.

Brisket Sold either on the bone or boned and rolled. Suitable for pot-roasting, braising or boiling, and often sold salted.

Thin ribs and thick ribs Usually sold boned and rolled. Good for braising and pot-roasts.

Silverside Traditionally salted and sold for boiling, though nowadays more often sold for roasting. (It needs constant basting.) Uncooked salted beef is grey, but turns pink during cooking.

Forerib The traditional cut of the roast beef of old England. Sold on the bone or boned and rolled for roasting.

Wing rib Roasting joint, but can be boned and sliced for frying or grilling.

Sirloin Prime roasting joint sold on the bone, with the fillet (the smaller 'eye' on the inside of the rib bone). The fillet can be removed and sold in slices as fillet steak, or whole to make the well-known dish, beef Wellington. The remainder of the sirloin is then boned by the butcher and sold as steaks. Boned rolled sirloin is also available for roasting.

Rump   Large, lean and tender cut, sold in slices for grilling or frying.

Topside   A popular lean cut with little or no fat, often sold with a layer of fat tied round it. Can be roasted or pot-roasted.

Steaks   These are slices of the most tender cuts of beef, for example:
Rump The joint next to the sirloin and one of the commonest cuts for grilling or frying. The 'point' is considered the best part for tenderness and flavour.
Fillet The undercut of the sirloin, probably one of the best-known and most expensive of the cuts used for grilling or frying. Very tender, though usually has less flavour than rump. The centre or eye of the fillet is considered the best part. The fillet is often cut and shaped into small rounds, known as 'tournedos'. A *filet mignon tournedos* is a small round steak, cut from the end of the fillet.
Chateaubriand A thick slice taken from the middle of the fillet, regarded as the most superb cut of all.
Sirloin This is cut into two parts. Porterhouse steak is cut from the thick end, giving a large juicy piece. When it is cooked on the bone it is called 'T-bone steak'. Minute steak is a very thin steak from the upper part of the sirloin, without any fat to trim off.
Entrecôte The part of the meat between the ribs of beef, though a slice cut from the sirloin or rump is also often sold under this name.
'Flash-fry' A term used for slices of lean cuts which have been passed between knife-covered rollers to make the meat more tender so that it can be fried quickly (flash-fried).

Lamb

The colour of lamb lean does not indicate eating quality, nor does the colour of the fat. There is a difference between the colour of new season's (often called spring) lamb and the meat from the larger older animals killed later in the year. New season's lamb is pale pink, tender and sweetly mild-tasting; older lamb is brownish-pink, although the colour can deepen as the season progresses. The fat in lamb should be crisp and white and there is usually very little gristle. Freshly cut surfaces should look slightly moist and the bones pinkish-white.

Because lamb is slaughtered young, before the connective tissues become tough, all the meat is tender. Check with the butcher that the lamb has been

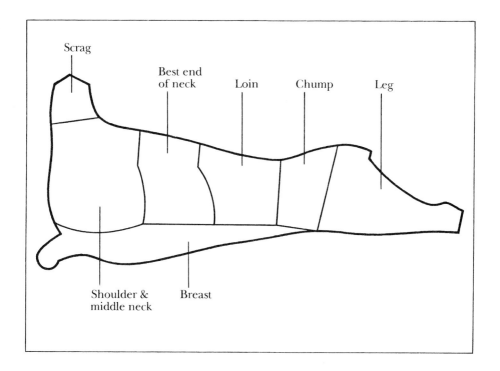

Scrag

Best end
of neck   Loin   Chump   Leg

Shoulder &   Breast
middle neck

correctly hung and aged – the usual time allowed for this is between four days and a week.

The first spring lamb is delicate and much in demand, which is reflected in its price. Prices fall as the season progresses and more lambs come on to the market. A few baby lambs are slaughtered for the specialist trade even before they are weaned. These are very expensive and must be specially ordered – the taste is remarkably sweet. A leg from a baby lamb will feed only two or three people.

Some specialist retailers and farms produce rare breeds of lamb, which fall into two groups – conventional and primitive. The conventional group contains such breeds as the famous Southdown and Ryland. The primitive breeds include Shetland, St Kilda and Soay – and a feral flock of seaweed-eating North Ronaldsay sheep with a distinctive taste and texture. All primitive breeds are small with very little fat cover: the meat is fine-grained and exceptionally tender with a full piquant flavour. In this case you may find that the lamb is hung for between two and three weeks to ensure prime flavour and tender meat. The lambs are reared in a non-intensive system, without the aid of growth-promoters.

Mutton – the meat of sheep aged 2–3 years – is difficult to buy at retail level. Only 15 per cent of all sheep become mutton and almost all are sold as ewe meat for meat products or to ethnic restaurants.

The names of lamb cuts vary in the regions: for instance, leg of lamb is known as 'gigot' in Scotland. Here are the most widely recognised names of cuts:

Shoulder   Used whole for roasting or braising. Can be boned, stuffed and rolled or sold on the bone. Can be halved into blade and knuckle ends, either of which can be roasted or braised. Boneless shoulder meat is suitable for cutting up for kebabs, casseroles, curries and pies as well as for mincing.

Scrag and middle neck   Traditional cuts for Lancashire hotpot and for Irish stew. Rather bony, inexpensive, usually sold as chops. The meat, trimmed of fat, is suitable for pies. Stock can be made from the bones. Middle neck can be braised. The main eye of meat from the middle neck is now sold as 'fillet of lamb' and is ideal for grilling.

Best end of neck   A whole roasting joint with six or seven rib bones. The butcher should remove or loosen the chine bone to make carving easier; this is sometimes known as rack of lamb. It may be roasted on the bone, or boned, stuffed and rolled. Two best end necks jointed together, specially prepared by the butcher, can be formed into 'crown of lamb' or 'guard of honour', for which he may make an extra charge. Cutlets from best end of neck with one rib bone to each are suitable for grilling or frying. A large best end can also be boned out, rolled, tied and cut into five or six 'noisettes' for grilling or frying.

Loin and chump   Loin can be roasted in the piece or boned, stuffed and rolled. The meat can also be divided into chops for grilling or frying. Chump chops, the most expensive, are recognisable by the small round piece of pelvic bone in them. (Leg or gigot chops have a small round bone in their centre.) The chump provides a useful small family joint.

Saddle of lamb   A large expensive roasting joint, this is the two loins still joined at the backbone. Double loin (or Barnsley chops) are cut from a saddle. These cuts will usually need to be ordered in advance.

Leg   A prime roasting joint for oven or spit-roasting. It can be boned and stuffed. A large leg is usually divided into fillet end and shank end, both suitable for roasting. Slices from the top of the fillet end are sometimes sold as leg steaks for grilling or frying. Shank end is suitable for braising.

Breast   A long thin cut, streaked with fat and lean, this can be boned, stuffed and rolled for an economical roast. Cut into 'riblets' on the bone, it can be grilled, barbecued or roasted in a similar way to pork spare-ribs.

Gammon, bacon and ham

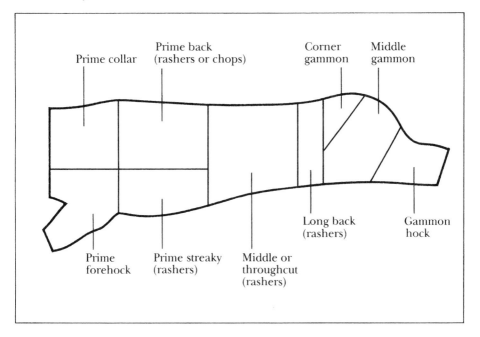

Bacon is preserved fresh pork meat, and milder and less salty than the original home-cured bacon. It is possible to buy home-cured bacon from some specialists, and it may need soaking before cooking. Over a hundred different curers in this country produce either loose or vacuum-packed varieties of bacon.

After the initial curing, the bacon may be smoked. In the case of the Wiltshire cure, the side of bacon is smoked whole. Other cuts, such as the middle, may be cured separately, with or without their bones. Unsmoked bacon is called 'green' and the rind is usually paler than that of smoked bacon. The fat should be moist (not wet), firm and white; the meat evenly coloured and sweet-smelling.

Strictly speaking, gammon is from the hind leg of the pig. When this hind leg has been cut from the whole carcass, separately cured and possibly smoked and matured, it becomes ham. There are many traditional cures and treatments: York ham is cured with dry salt and lightly smoked; Bradenham ham is cured in a similar way, then pickled in molasses for a month which makes the skin turn black; Wiltshire ham is a mild cure; and Suffolk ham is sweet-cured in beer and sugar or molasses, with a strong smoky flavour.

Look for butchers and farm shops, increasing in number, which sell organically produced bacons and hams, prepared and smoked on the premises (see page 218 for addresses).

The cuts are as follows:

Corner gammon   Small, economical, triangular; can be boiled to serve hot or cold.

Middle gammon   Prime, lean, meaty: good for boiling, braising, baking. Gammon rashers or steaks can be cut from it for grilling or frying.

Gammon hock   Knuckle end; gives succulent meat for casseroles, soups, pies.

Prime forehock   Good all-rounder for boiling or to cube for casseroles; can also be minced.

Prime collar   Economical rashers. As a joint, may need to be soaked, but good for boiling, braising.

Prime streaky   Economical as joint or rashers. Rashers suitable for grilling, frying, lining pâté dishes, for chopping or mincing. Joint is excellent to have boiled, pressed and cold.

Prime back   Joint, rashers, chops. Usually sold as rashers or boneless chops. Thick pieces good for boiling or braising.

Middle or throughcut   Back and streaky together, giving a long rasher for grilling or frying or a tasty joint for boiling or baking (excellent stuffed).

Pork

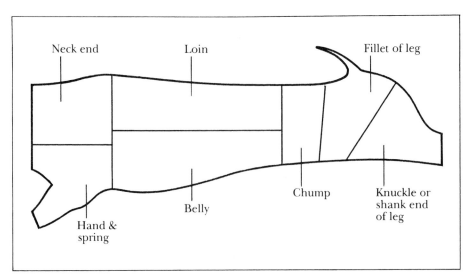

Pork lean should be very pale pink (almost colourless) and firm, and the freshly cut surface should be slightly moist. The fat should be firm and white; the skin pale and dry.

Some specialist butchers and farms produce traditional breeds of pigs – such as Middle Whites, Gloucester Old Spots, Tamworths and Berkshires – in a non-intensive system, without the aid of growth-promoters and using additive-free feeds. These animals take longer to mature, thus producing a carcass of superior quality, texture and flavour.

As there is no standard method of carcass cutting, there can be regional variations, as there can also be in the names of cuts. The cuts are as follows:

Neck end (spare-rib and blade bone)   A large economical roasting joint that can be boned, stuffed and rolled. Can be divided into blade bone and spare-rib, both suitable for roasting, braising, stewing. Spare-rib chops can be braised, grilled or fried. Spare-rib is suitable for pie filling.

Hand and spring   A large roasting joint that can be divided into hand and shank. Both are suitable for casseroles and stews.

Belly   An economical cut that can be boned, stuffed, rolled and roasted or boiled, and coated in breadcrumbs to serve cold. Belly slices are ideal for an inexpensive grill and the bones ('spare-ribs') with a little meat left on are excellent when marinated and grilled or barbecued. American-style spare-ribs are removed in one piece, leaving the meat between the rib bones; Chinese-style spare-ribs are separate bones with a very small amount of meat on them.

Leg   Often used whole as a celebratory joint. Can be cut into four or more succulent roasting joints. Often cut into the fillet end and knuckle end. The fillet end, which is the top of the leg, is a prime piece, good boned and stuffed; it can also be sliced into steaks for grilling, frying or braising.

Trotters   The feet are usually salted and boiled or used to make brawn. Good for stuffing and grilling.

Loin   A good roast on the bone (the butcher should remove or loosen the chine bone to make carving easier) or boned, stuffed and rolled. Can be divided into loin and chump chops for grilling or frying. Sometimes the loin chops are sold with the kidney attached. Produces good crackling.

Tenderloin   A tender lean cut found underneath the backbone of the loin, in the same position as the beef fillet. It is sometimes called 'pork fillet', but should not be confused with the fillet at the end of the leg. Usually sliced for frying, cubed for kebabs, stuffed and tied for roasting or braising.

Poultry and game

There is an old-fashioned picture-book idea of poultry as birds bred and nurtured in the farmyard, and game birds as totally wild and faintly exotic. However, the truth is that wild, semi-wild and domestic (cross-bred, hybrid, free-range, deep litter and intensively reared) types overlap. Guinea fowl and quail, for instance, were once truly game birds, but are now farmed commercially and may be termed 'poultry'. Wild game birds shot in the rough include mallard, teal, pigeon, snipe, greylag goose and so on. Semi-wild or hand-reared birds include pheasant and some partridge.

Rabbit (furred game) may be domesticated or wild, whereas hare are considered too highly strung and sensitive for hand-rearing. Deer, not yet domesticated animals, are usually farmed in open fields and parkland; however, they are now under threat of intensive farming systems. Until a recent Act of Parliament, deer were not transported to an abattoir for slaughter because their nature, needs and temperament were thought to render them too sensitive to endure the traumatic atmosphere of the slaughterhouse.

It is thought that a large proportion of our game is exported to Europe, where the British policy of game conservation is greatly envied. Ironically, as game is enjoying a revival as a flavoursome, natural and healthy food, some species are declining because of the effect of modern farming methods on their habitat and environment. What's more, it would be difficult to guarantee nowadays that even the wildest of game birds had not been affected by herbicides and pesticides used on the farmlands where they may feed. Other countries have different attitudes to and categories of game. Thrushes (protected in this country), robins, blackbirds, bullfinches and other small birds are roasted or grilled in Italy, and thrush pâté is a French delicacy. Raccoon, squirrel, woodchuck and beaver – along with muskrat and moose – are among the hunted game animals of America.

The flesh of nearly all poultry and game is appealing because of its low fat content. Inevitably, such lean meat will tend to dryness or toughness when cooked unsympathetically. Tenderness and succulence can be achieved by identifying the age and culinary characteristics of the bird or beast, choosing the correct cooking method (see page 35) and, in the case of game, careful hanging. Most types of game are extremely rich in potassium, phosphorus and sulphur and also contain significant amounts of other minerals important in our diet.

Shopping for poultry

The descriptions on the packaging of poultry on sale in the shops can be quite confusing. 'Fresh', for instance, does not mean 'free-range': 'free-range' denotes birds that have freedom of movement outdoors, have a longer maturing time before slaughter and, in some cases, a superior diet to that of the average broiler/roaster. It is undoubtedly the longer maturing time and exercise that contributes to the better taste and texture of these 'free-rangers', but the number of birds to the acre is still fairly high.

Shopping for, hanging and storing game

If you are new to the gloriously robust and wild taste of game, it might be best to start by sampling guinea fowl, pheasant or rabbit and progressing gently from there. Even those few people with a plentiful supply of game and a bulging game larder will admit that a little of the richness of game goes a long way.

Some supermarkets and food halls now sell fresh and frozen oven-ready grouse, partridge, woodcock and pheasant. Otherwise, game is available from licensed butchers and poulterers, and in some areas direct from farms or estates. If the game is in the feather, the retailer will advise you whether it has been correctly hung. Hanging is most important, and below suggested hanging times are given for the various types of game together with their seasons. It is permitted to buy fresh game up to 10 days after the end of its open season. Frozen game, if legally caught, may be purchased all the year round from licensed game dealers.

In general, when shopping for game birds, bear in mind that younger ones are more tender and very slightly milder, and may be roasted in the traditional manner. The breast will need protection (usually with bacon) during cooking to prevent it from drying out. Older birds are suitable for slow-cooking stews and casseroles.

A bird that is hung and drawn may be stored in the refrigerator for 2 days. If it is to be frozen, game should have a slightly shorter hanging time than if it is to be eaten fresh. Most game should be stored in the freezer for no more than 6 months, although lean cuts will keep for up to 9 months.

Tenderness and flavour are the two main reasons for hanging game. The fibres of the flesh break down and the meat becomes more tender, as each individual bird's characteristic gamy flavour is intensified. There are no hard and fast times for the length of hanging, as this depends on weather conditions and personal taste. Moreover, if you buy a bird in feather from a licensed game dealer, you should ask if it is already well hung or requires further hanging. Another consideration is the age and sex of the bird, and again, only an experienced game dealer or expert will be able to advise you. Beware of overhung flesh, which will have blueish patches on it. In general, birds are ready when the feathers on the breast or tail can be plucked out with ease. Game birds are generally hung from the neck, and this should be done in a cool, shaded and well ventilated area. If the weather is warm and humid they should be hung for the shortest recommended period – and longer when the weather is cold.

Bear in mind too, that personal taste is a consideration. Some people like their game quite high: others may prefer a less pronounced flavour. Birds are always hung unviscerated and in feather. It is important to get them cooled down and hung as soon as possible after the shoot. Game birds or animals which may have become rather sniffy – for instance, if they have been wrapped in plastic and travelled in a car boot – can be first plucked or skinned and then washed in a mild solution of water and vinegar or water and Milton. When plucking a bird that is not well hung and so has rather stubborn feathers, it is helpful to immerse the bird briefly in boiling water first. Remaining stubble may be singed off over a gas flame or candle.

Game Birds, Hares and Rabbits

Game Average weight	Servings	Hanging time	Oven temperatures Roasting times approx.	Shooting seasons
Wild Duck				
Mallard 2½–2¾ lb (1.1–1.3 kg)	2–3	Up to 2 days	gas mark 8, 450°F (230°C) 20–30 minutes	below coastal high tide mark 1 Sept to 20 Feb
Teal 11–13 oz (300–375 g)	1		gas mark 7, 425°F (220°C) 10–15 minutes	Inland 1 Sept to 31 Jan
Widgeon 1½–2 lb	2		gas mark 7, 425°F (220°C) 15–25 minutes	
Geese				
Pink-footed 6–7 lb (2.7–3.3 kg)	6	1–2 days	Young goose gas mark 7, 425°F (220°C) 10 minutes	as for duck
Greylag 8–10 lb	6	1–2 days	gas mark 3, 325°F (170°C) 1 hour Old goose braise or stew	
Woodpigeon				
1–1¼ lb (450–550 g)	1		gas mark 7, 425°F (220°C) 20 minutes	no close season

Shin of beef stewed with herbed dumplings (page 68), and Pork cooked in milk (page 106)

Game Average weight	Servings	Hanging time	Oven temperatures Roasting times approx.	Shooting seasons
Quail				
	1		gas mark 5, 375°F (190°C) 15–20 minutes	no close season
Hares				
6½–7 lb (3–3.2 kg)	6–10	1 week**	young hare, gas mark 6, 400°F (200°C) 20 minutes per lb (450 g) older hare gas mark 2, 300°F (150°C) 1½–2 hours	no close season but they may not be offered for sale during Mar to Jul inclusive
Rabbits				
2½–3½ lb (1.1–1.6 kg)	3		gas mark 6, 400°F (200°C) 1 hour	no close season
Grouse				
1¼–1½ lb (550–700 g)	1–2	3–10 days	gas mark 5, 375°F (190°C) 35 minutes	12 Aug to 10 Dec
Partridge cock 13–15 oz (375–425 g) hen 12½–14½ oz (360–410 g)	1–2	5–12 days	gas mark 7, 425°F (220°C) 30 minutes	1 Sept to 1 Feb
Pheasant cock 3–3½ lb (1.4–1.6 kg) hen 2–2½ lb (900 g–1.1 kg)	4	3–14 days	gas mark 5, 375°F (190°C) ¾–1 hour	1 Oct to 1 Feb
Common Snipe				
	1–2 per person	up to 6 days*	gas mark 8, 450°F (230°C) 6–15 minutes	12 Aug to 31 Jan
Woodcock				
	1	up to 6 days***	gas mark 7, 425°F (220°C) 15–20 minutes	England–Wales 1 Oct to 31 Jan Scotland 1 Sept to 31 Jan

* Information supplied by *The Game Conservancy*. (More information available, see page 218.)
** Hang from hind legs with dish under head to catch the blood.
*** Watch carefully as usually supplied and cooked with entrails intact.

Cornish pasty (page 72), and Lamb's kidneys in baked potatoes (page 96)

There *are*, however, humane producers of quality free-range poultry. They ensure 'high welfare' conditions, an environment as near as possible to the bird's natural one, and avoid using antibiotics. Transportation is in specially designed trailers to avoid stress and crushing. Slaughter is by electrical stunning first, then by hand. There is concern that, in highly intensive poultry-rearing systems, a proportion of birds are not effectively stunned and killed, and may be conveyed live to the bleeding, boiling-water and plucking stage.

Fresh poultry costs more than frozen because of the cost of handling stocks of freshly killed birds which deteriorate rapidly. Frozen poultry will suffer some loss of flavour and moisture as a result of 'drip' (see page 20). When shopping for fresh, plucked and drawn birds, buy only those whose skin is soft, smooth and dry to the touch (wet skin indicates that they may have been frozen); the colour should be even and the flesh plump and loose with some elasticity, not tight and hard. The legs should be pliable. Fresh birds are also sold plucked but with the head and feet still attached and the innards intact – and these birds are considered by many to have the best flavour.

With regard to buying free-range poultry, it is best to put your trust in butchers of integrity and good reputation. Otherwise you may be able to buy direct from some farm outlets (see page 218 for addresses and information). In supermarkets and general food shops look for the British Quality Mark or EEC identification mark. Without these symbols on the package, you may be buying an imported frozen bird (with an English-sounding brand name) of unspecified origin and quality.

When buying frozen poultry, check that there are no broken limbs or bruising: these may indicate inferior quality and poor handling. Ensure that the packaging is undamaged.

Storing poultry

Unwrap fresh poultry before storing – it will sweat and become damp in non-porous plastic and there is a danger of bacterial growth. (If there are giblets, remove them and store them in a separate container, although it is better to cook them straight away as they have a comparatively short storage time.) Cover the bird with greaseproof paper, butter paper or aluminium foil and store it in the refrigerator for no more than 4 days at a temperature no higher than 35°F (2°C). If the bird is ready-stuffed, it should be used within 2 days. If you are storing it in a cool larder, do not keep it for longer than 24 hours. Avoid cross-contamination: do not store poultry with fish or other meats.

When packing any fresh poultry for the freezer, first prepare and, if necessary, draw the bird. Truss it and cover any protruding bones with foil or a double thickness of greaseproof paper, then pack it in a polythene bag, getting rid of as much surplus air as possible. Seal, label and date. Thaw in the wrapping.

Unless you intend to cook it straight after purchase, poultry bought ready-frozen should be transferred from the retailer to the home freezer as quickly as possible to avoid the danger of thawing. No bird should be re-frozen. Read the storing instructions on the packaging before you commit the bird to the freezer. It is not recommended that birds should be stuffed before being frozen: the herbs and seasonings used in the stuffing can develop a rather unpleasant flavour after about 3 months and there is a risk that in the eventual cooking the stuffing might not be thoroughly heated through, thus possibly constituting a health hazard.

Ideally, you should plan ahead and defrost frozen poultry in the refrigerator, first puncturing the seal of the bag. As with any uncooked meat, do not allow the juices from uncooked fresh or frozen poultry to drip on to other foods while storing and preparing.

Always ensure that poultry is thoroughly defrosted before cooking. Check that there are no ice crystals in the cavity, and that the legs and thighs are soft and flexible. Cook thoroughly and, if stuffing is to be served, cook the stuffing separately, or stuff the neck cavity only.

Cooked poultry that is to be frozen should be cooled as quickly as possible and never frozen with the stuffing inside.

It is vital that the storage practices recommended in this section for uncooked chicken are followed if the risk of salmonella infection is to be avoided. Salmonella is a bacterium widely prevalent in the environment. It may be found in water and soil, where birds and animals feed, in the intestinal tract of about 3 per cent of human beings, and in all other animals and birds.

Because it is prevalent in nature, salmonella may also be present in raw food such as meat, fish, poultry, eggs, unpasteurised milk and raw vegetables. Some chicken, like all meat and many other raw foods, may contain salmonella. However, salmonella is easily destroyed by heat and therefore, even if present in food, it can be completely eliminated by proper cooking, and by following good food handling and storing practices.

Chicken

The intensification of chicken production has resulted, by and large, in flesh with a flavour (if any) far removed from that of the rarely found genuine free-range farmyard bird. At the turn of the century, and after many years of research and development in breeding special strains, three main types of chicken were eventually established: egg layers, table birds and those suitable for general purposes. It was from then onwards that commercial poultry farming began.

At the time of writing, it is estimated that each *week* nearly five million chickens in fresh or frozen form, as well as the equivalent of a further two million birds in fresh or frozen portions, are bought from retail outlets. A further three million chickens are supplied to the catering market each week, and up to another million go for processing into products such as chicken burgers, prepared pies and chilled recipe dishes in various sauces. The popularity and sales of chicken – especially in portions – are steadily increasing: the most commonly bought broiler/roaster being inexpensive, versatile and preferred by slimmers, those who are trying to cut down on fatty meats, and those who are turning away from red meat.

Buying a whole chicken – even for two people – is usually the best option. It is more economical, and you can easily cut it up yourself to your own requirements. The carcass and trimmings will make good stock. Ask for the giblets, although they are not always available with fresh chicken. Old-fashioned giblet pie is good, and the giblets are good for stock but do not use the liver in this as it adds a bitter taste.

For frozen chicken the following is a guide to storage times:

Ready-frozen chicken	3 months
Fresh chicken	1 year
Boiling fowl	9 months
Giblets	3 months
Cooked chicken	2 months

To thaw, follow the general instructions for poultry on page 35. A 3 lb (1.5 kg) bird will take about 32 hours to thaw in the refrigerator and 9 hours at room temperature.

The following types of chicken are those most commonly found on sale:

Broiler/roasting chickens Young hens or cockerels, approximately seven weeks old. According to the British Chicken Information Service, broilers are fed on a diet of wheat, soya, vegetable oil, vitamins and minerals. The BCIS confirms that bonemeal is also used. These birds are best for roasting or poaching (they are very tender), but all cooking methods are suitable. A bunch of fresh herbs – especially rosemary or thyme – half a lemon or a piece of carrot and onion placed inside the cavity will give a pleasant aroma, although will not make an appreciable difference to the *taste* of the meat. To ensure even and thorough cooking of the chicken, stuffing should be in the neck cavity or cooked separately. Roast at 20 minutes to the lb (450 g) plus 20 minutes extra at gas mark 6, 400°F (200°C). Always test to ensure that the chicken is cooked through by piercing the thigh with a skewer: the juices should run golden and clear, not pink. Also gently pull the leg away from the body: if it gives, the bird is ready.

Free-range chickens   These are generally introduced to free-range conditions when they are old enough to stand up to the elements, and their diet and longer growing period gives them a firm texture and fuller flavour. They are also fed on a diet of wheat, soya, vegetable oil, vitamins and minerals. Best for roasting (as above), but all cooking methods are suitable.

Corn-fed chickens   These cost more because of their diet of maize, grains, proteins, minerals and vitamins. The natural golden colour of their flesh comes from the maize in their food, and it is said that they have a distinctive creamy taste, but this is a matter of opinion. They are best for roasting (as above) and poaching, though all cooking methods are suitable.

Poulets noirs   Black-feathered birds from south-western France. According the British Chicken Information Service, they are fed a natural, high-protein, additive-free cereal diet which includes wheat, soya and other grain proteins together with vitamins and minerals. The birds are recognisable by their black hocks and high breast-bone, rather like a guinea fowl's. They have a mild gamy taste and firm texture. This is due to their diet and longer growing period – they take over twice as long as a standard white chicken to reach a given weight.

Poussins   These are baby chickens, weighing 1–1¼ lb (450–550 g). One will serve one to two people. They may be split and grilled, barbecued, or stuffed and roasted. They have little flavour, so when cooking them use herbs and spices with enthusiasm.

Boiling fowls   Usually egg layers past their cost-effective laying performance, these may weigh anything from 2½–7 lb (1.25–3 kg). As their name suggests, they are best for boiling or slow stewing and casseroling. They have more flavour and their texture is prone to be stringier and tougher than that of birds bred for the table. Small skinny boilers are available in some areas where there is demand from ethnic populations or restaurants.

Capons   These are young cockerels that have been castrated and specially fattened to 5–8 lb (2.25–3.5 kg) and are very rarely available. They have pale, rich livers. Another method of producing capons is by injecting their necks with hormone capsules – now illegal in this country. You may find 'capon-style' birds on sale: these are simply large roasting birds with a plump breast.

Chicken portions These may be halves or quarters. I do not like frozen chicken quarters: they appear to be frozen birds, sawn into four in a random way producing unattractive chunks containing bits of this and that. The labels often do not specify their origin.

Breasts These are available on the bone, boned out, with or without skin, fresh, chilled or frozen. They may also be available as fillets and escalopes, and vary in size.

Supremes These are a French cut of breast sold with the wing bone attached.

Legs or thighs and drumsticks These are the dark-meat portions which may be baked, fried, grilled or casseroled.

Wings These are good for grilling.

Chicken livers Available in tubs, fresh or frozen: check the label for origin. They have a distinctive flavour and are good for stir-frying. (See Risotto with Chicken Livers and Fennel, page 128.)

Duck

Frozen and chilled fresh oven-ready ducklings are increasingly popular. A few specialist poulterers and markets also sell 'fresh-plucked' ducklings with the head and feet still attached but which have not been eviscerated.

Duck production in this country is highly advanced and we export duck breeding stock and technology to over seventy countries, including China where Britain is now the largest supplier. Our table birds are reared from the hybrid strains developed at Cherry Valley Farms in Lincolnshire. One of the most sought-after is the CV Super-M. Sounding and performing somewhat like a motor car, this bird has a low feed conversion ratio: hence its success.

Smaller free-range poultry farms produce ducks with more familiar names such as Aylesbury, Barbary and Muscovy, and some less well-known like Cornvale and Khaki Campbell. These are available from good poulterers and the food halls of large stores or direct from farm retail outlets. They may be oven-ready whole birds, jointed or in supremes.

In general, the rules for cooking duck depart somewhat from those for chicken and turkey. It is popular to serve the breast quite rare and pink (see, for example, Simple Duck Breasts with Apple Sauce, page 142). Duck is fatty and naturally self-basting, so needs no extra oil for roasting. Wash and dry the bird thoroughly and use a fork or skewer to make deep pricks all over the skin, but do not puncture the flesh. Place on a trivet or rack set over a deep roasting tin. Roast at gas mark 7, 425°F (220°C) for 10–15 minutes, depending on the size of the bird, then turn the oven down to gas mark 4, 350°F (180°C), and continue to cook, allowing 15–20 minutes per lb (450 g). You will need to allow about 2 lb (900 g) weight per person as the fat content of duck is high and most of it runs out during roasting. A 6 lb (2.75 kg) bird should serve four people: it is a good idea to buy two smaller birds to serve more.

Turkey

There is a trend to smaller turkeys to match the decline in family size. Fresh free-range turkeys have a longer maturing time, a stronger flavour and firmer flesh than frozen birds – which may have been fattened fast and killed young to achieve tender, moist and delicately flavoured meat. Hen birds are reckoned to be plumper and more flavoursome than cocks.

Many turkeys are reared to Traditional Farm Fresh Turkey Association standards and are humanely slaughtered, hand-plucked and hung before evisceration for a minimum of 7 days for greater flavour and tenderness.

When it comes to cooking turkey, apply the same golden rules used for chicken (apart from the oven temperature; which is lower for turkey), paying special attention to correct thawing. The British Turkey Federation has provided the following guidelines for thawing and cooking:

Thawing and cooking times for whole turkeys and portions

Oven-ready weight including stuffing	Approx. thawing time at room temperature 70°F (21°C)	Approx. cooking time for uncovered birds with or without stuffing, gas mark 4, 350°F (180°C)	Approx. cooking time for foil roast at gas mark 4, 350°F (180°C)
1¼ lb (550 g)*	4 hours	1½ hours	1¾ hours
2 lb (900 g)*	9 hours	1½ hours	1¾ hours
3 lb (1.4 kg)*	10 hours	1¾ hours	2 hours
4 lb (1.8 kg)*	12 hours	1¾ hours	2¼ hours
5 lb (2.3 kg)	15 hours	2 hours	2½ hours
10 lb (4.5 kg)	18 hours	3 hours	3½ hours
15 lb (6.75 kg)	24 hours	3¾ hours	4¾ hours

* These smaller weights represent large turkey drumsticks or turkey roasts, both suitable to roast for small numbers.

Goose

Goose used to be traditional fare at Christmas before turkey became popular and cheaper. Michaelmas was also a traditional time to eat this bird, in celebration of the harvest. Goose is now enjoying a rapidly expanding market, although it is still regarded as a luxury food. Many small producers rear their geese on free-range pasture, feeding them on natural foods, grass, corn and root crops.

Free-range geese are available fresh – either long-legged (that is, plucked but not eviscerated and with head and feet still attached) or oven-ready – or frozen. At 6 months of age, goslings off the pasture will have had a much longer maturing time than chicken, duck and turkey; older birds are also available but these are likely to be on the tough side. Although goose is available from good butchers, poulterers and some food halls and supermarkets, it will normally have to be ordered in advance. Its 'season' runs from September through to Christmastime, but a limited number of birds are available throughout the year, especially at Easter.

When choosing a frozen goose, check that both bird and packaging are undamaged, and buy in plenty of time for it to thaw out thoroughly. When buying a fresh-plucked goose, a young bird may be recognised by the pliable under-bill, supple wind pipe and soft legs and feet.

To store a hung, plucked, drawn and trussed goose, remove any wrappings and elastic bands, take out the giblets and pull the neck flap back over the bird's breast. If possible, put the bird breast down on a rack in the coldest part of the refrigerator with a container underneath to catch any drips of blood or liquid. (If liquid collects in the bird's cavity, carefully tip it away.) Cover the bird with greaseproof paper to prevent the flesh from becoming dry. Store in this way for no longer than 3 days.

The older and fattier a goose, the shorter the time it can be stored in the freezer. It is best to remove, wrap and store the giblets separately. Goose fat should be stored in small quantities: flexible ice-cube trays make useful containers as you may often need just a knob or two. The following are recommended maximum storage times for frozen goose:

Young goose	4–6 months
Goose giblets	2 months
Cooked goose	1 month
Goose fat	3 months

The thawing time for frozen goose is similar to that for turkey (page 39).

Geese range in weight from about 7 lb (3 kg) to as much as 15 lb (6.75 kg). As a general rule when buying an oven-ready bird, allow 1 lb (450 g) per person, but a larger quantity when purchasing a small goose as the ratio of meat to bone is smaller. The meat is rich and flavoursome, and the bird should not normally need basting since it is fatty. To prepare a goose for cooking, follow the general guidelines for duck on page 38, ensuring that you wash and dry the bird thoroughly both inside and out beforehand. Make gravy from the giblets, which can also be used (along with left-over meat) for pâté.

Goose can be quick- or slow-roasted. For the former (suitable only for young birds), cook in a pre-heated oven at gas mark 6, 400°F (200°C), allowing 15 minutes per lb (450 g) plus an extra 15 minutes. To slow-roast, cook in a pre-heated oven at gas mark 4, 350°F (180°C), allowing 20 minutes per lb (450 g) and 20 minutes over. See Roast Goose on page 144 for the semi-braising method.

The goose carcass can be boiled to make excellent stock. Left-over goose meat is excellent in salad, in coarse pâté or with pasta.

Guinea fowl

Not so long ago, guinea fowl were classed as game. Now they are farmed commercially and have a less 'wild' taste – something in between that of chicken and pheasant. I was surprised to learn that the man responsible for first raising, packaging and popularising the guinea fowl is the Danish pianist and humorist, Victor Borge.

Guinea fowl are available all the year round, but are at their best from February to June. Buy them from a quality butcher, poulterer, game dealer or good supermarket. They are generally sold young and very fresh – like chicken – rather than well hung. Many are reared in Belgium. Guinea fowl are also available direct from some speciality poultry farms. If you are buying them in the feather, look for plenty of healthy grey feathers spotted with white. Ideally they should be hung for 2 days in cool weather, but for a shorter period if it is warm. Follow the general guidelines for fresh chicken (page 34) when storing.

Guinea fowl are light-boned, so even what might appear to be a small bird will have a good proportion of meat. An average-sized bird – about 3 lb (1.4 kg) – will feed four people. The flesh is tender but the breast tends to dryness. Recipes and methods of cooking for pheasant and chicken are also suitable for guinea fowl.

Cooking game

There are many opinions about cooking game, and it is probably best to be guided by individual recipes, the age of the bird or animal, and by basic commonsense and instinct.

Gamebirds

Identifying the age of game birds can be difficult in some cases. In general, young birds have soft-textured feet and older birds coarser darker feet and, in the case of cock birds, larger spurs. The breast should be plump and the breast bone pliable. In the partridge the outer flight feathers will give an approximate indication of age: a young bird has pointed flight feathers while in an older bird these are rounded. This is not the case with pheasant, however, where estimating the age is a subject best left to the specialist. In other birds, such as geese, indications of age are the differences in markings on the breast or wing feathers of juveniles and mature birds and in the colouration of the bill, legs and head. See the chart on pages 32–33 for estimated cooking times.

Though usually accepted as game, pigeons are usually classified as vermin and there is no close season. As they are plumpest when they have been living off farmland, they are best between May and October. However, they are available all year round. A young pigeon will have softer, pinker legs than an older bird, and will have a good fat breast. Woodpigeons are probably best for eating: the adult birds are distinguishable by the white ring around the neck. It is recommended that pigeons are hung for a short time (2–3 days), head downwards (unlike other game birds) so that the flesh does not become too dark.

Quails are now also farmed and sometimes regarded as poultry. There is no close season. You will need one or two birds for each person, and in general they may be roasted at gas mark 5, 375°F (190°C), for 15–20 minutes. They may be stuffed, but are best boned out for this treatment. Quails are also good poached or quickly casseroled. The flavour is delicate, and they are usually hung for no more than 1 day – though up to 3 will improve the flavour. The carcass makes good stock.

Rabbit and hare

Farmed rabbits have a milder flavour and more tender flesh than wild rabbits, which *must* be young for good results. There are several signs to look for in both wild rabbits and hares that indicate a young animal. The ears of young hares (leverets) and rabbits should tear easily. The animals should be plump and have nice small white pointed teeth: the more cracked and yellow-brown the teeth are, the older the rabbit or hare. If the pelt is scruffy and the body is hard, this will also indicate an old animal. Old hares and rabbits are useful for pâtés or terrines and will be improved by overnight marinating. See individual recipes for the various cooking methods.

Venison

In general venison, the meat of deer, should be dark and close-grained, the fat white and firm. Young venison (about 18 months old) may have only 5 per cent fat, whereas a fully mature stag of over 5 years may have up to 20 per cent fat at the end of a good summer – but half of this fat is composed of polyunsaturates. All the fat is on the surface, and there is no marbling. The taste, texture and tenderness or otherwise of venison is largely determined by correct ageing and hanging.

Of the wild and park deer available, it is generally considered that roe deer are the best and most reliable in terms of taste and tenderness. Next come fallow deer; in these the meat tends to be slightly darker and there is a little more fat. The red deer, found mainly in the Scottish Highlands, cannot be relied on to produce good results when cooked unless you can be absolutely certain of its age. In young deer there is no difference in taste and texture between buck and doe.

Most of us will buy venison ready hung and prepared from a butcher or licensed game dealer. It will usually have been hung from 3 days to 2 weeks, depending on the age, sex, breed, feeding habits and habitat of the animal. For these reasons, as well as those of personal taste, it is not possible to give an accurate chart of cooking times and methods, as each cut and type of venison will need different considerations. It is best to be guided by the advice given by your dealer, or by individual recipes.

Because of its leanness, venison tends to dryness and joints will need some protection when roasting. Marinating joints will not make much difference as marinades cannot penetrate right through the meat. A good old-fashioned method of protecting and lubricating the flesh is to wrap the joint in a good suet crust. Aluminium foil does not work so well – it seems to be too 'hard' a method. Larding is a traditional way of keeping venison moist during cooking: it involves inserting strips of pork fat either with a larding needle or by making slits in the meat and pushing in the strips with a skewer. Pieces of cut-up venison for stews and so on may be marinated with appreciable effect. Steaks and fillets for grilling can be simply brushed with olive oil. Never overcook or cook these under too fierce a heat: err on the side of undercooking as they will continue to cook when removed from the heat; othewise they will be dry and dull. In general the cooking of venison differs from that of other meat and it is advisable to follow individual recipes or seek advice from a knowledgeable licensed butcher or game dealer.

Venison: Seasons

Roe Deer	England	Scotland	Weight
Buck	1 April to 31 October	1 May to 20 October	38–50 lb (17–22 kg)
Doe	1 November to 28/29 February	21 October to 28/29 February	33–45 lb (15–20 kg) (but there is considerable variation in locality)

Fallow Deer	England	Scotland	Weight
Wild Buck	1 August to	1 August to	9–10 stone (57–65 kg)
Park Buck	30 April	30 April	10–15 stone (65–95 kg), cleaned, and in good condition
Wild Doe	1 November to	21 October to	6 stone (38 kg)
Park Doe	28/29 February	15 February	7–8 stone (40–44 kg), in good condition

Red Deer	England	Scotland	Weight
Wild Stag	1 August to	1 July to	14–16 stone (89–101 kg), cleaned (Scotland) up to 32 stone (200 kg) in England
Park Stag	30 April	20 October	16–24 stone (101–52 kg), depending on amount of available food
Wild Hind	1 November to	21 October to	7½–11 stone (42–70 kg), cleaned
Park Hind	28/29 February	15 February	10–15 stone (65–95 kg), depending on amount of available food

Sika Deer	England	Scotland	Weight
Stag	1 August to 30 April	1 August to 30 April	7–8 stone (40–50 kg), cleaned
Hind	1 November to 28/29 February	21 October to 15 February	5–6 stone (30–35 kg), cleaned

Offal

Offal is not to everyone's taste. I think its image suffers because of its name – the word 'offal' derives from 'off-fall', describing those parts of pigs, sheep and cattle which are cut away from the carcass when it is prepared for sale. Most kinds of offal are delicious to eat, and extremely nutritious.

Offal should be eaten only when very fresh: it should be cooked on the day of purchase. Alternatively, it may be frozen, but this too should be done on the day of purchase. Offal may be stored in the freezer for 3 months; frozen home-made dishes containing offal for 1 month. If you buy ready-frozen offal, never·re-freeze it once it has begun to thaw.

Brains　There are three kinds of brains sold for human consumption: calf's (the best), lamb's and ox's. They are sold in sets – a set of lamb's brains serves one, and a set of calf's or ox brains serves two. Buy and prepare brains when they are absolutely fresh: they should look shiny, plump and moist, be pinkish grey in colour and smell fresh. The membrane from fresh brains should slip easily from the meat; if they are not fresh, it will stick in the crevices. To prepare, soak for a couple of hours in cold water to remove all traces of blood. Remove the arteries and membranes with a sharp pointed knife, cover with water and parboil for 5–15 minutes, depending on size. Two tablespoons vinegar or lemon juice can be added to each 2 pints (1.1 litres) water to help retain the pale colour. Add other ingredients for flavour, such as a whole onion or bay leaf if required. After parboiling, plunge into cold water or allow to cool in the cooking liquid, to firm the meat before using in the chosen recipe. Cooked brains have a delicate flavour and creamy texture.

Caul　Pig's caul is the lace-like membrane around the paunch – it is used as the 'skin' for faggots and other forcemeat sausages.

Chitterlings　These are pig's intestines – opaque, white and with a plaited appearance. They are good for grilling and frying. Chitterlings are available only in certain regions.

Feet　There are three kinds: pig's trotters, calf's feet and cow heel. Pig's and calf's feet are gelatinous and make wonderful jellied stock; trotters may also be boned, stuffed and roasted or grilled (see the recipe on page 118). Cow heel is available in certain regions only and is used mainly for broth.

Head   Pig's (the best) or calf's heads, whole or halved, are used to make brawn. Sheep's heads may be used for the same purpose but preparing them is more fiddly. Pig's cheeks, boiled and coated in egg and breadcrumbs, are sold as Bath chaps. Pig's and calf's ears may be grilled.

Heart   There are four kinds: ox's, calf's, lamb's and pig's. Ox heart – a whole one can weigh up to 6 lb (2.75 kg) – needs long slow cooking; it should be served sliced. Calf's heart is much smaller and more tender: it may be roasted, braised, stewed or casseroled. Lamb's and pig's hearts are excellent stuffed and then roasted or braised. They can also be cut up and fried or casseroled.

Kidney   There are four kinds: ox's, calf's, lamb's and pig's. Ox and calf's kidneys are many-lobed, elongated, coarse and have a strong flavour. They are traditionally used in casseroles and pies. Lamb's kidneys, the most popular, are the smallest of all and are tender and well-flavoured: they are suitable for grilling and frying. Pig's kidneys can be soaked in milk for a milder flavour and are suitable when halved or cut into pieces for grilling and frying. One calf's kidney will serve two people, but allow 2 lamb's kidneys and 1 pig's kidney per person. Kidneys are sold either in their suet (protective fat) or loose. They should smell mild and pleasant and be smooth and clean-looking.

Liver   The best liver is calf's, followed by lamb's, pig's and ox's (coarse and strong-flavoured). Calf's, lamb's and pig's liver can be grilled, fried or used in braised dishes. When frying or grilling liver, cook it briskly so that the inside is still pink – overcooked liver becomes dry and tough. Pig's and ox livers are mainly used in stews and casseroles or minced for pâtés and stuffings. The strong flavour of pig's liver can be mellowed by soaking for an hour or two in milk; ox liver should be soaked overnight.

Lungs   Known more often as 'lights', these are not a common food in this country but are used in forcemeats or in casseroles.

Marrowbone   This is the bone of the shoulder or thigh of an ox or calf. Sawn into short cylinders, it should be boiled whole and served in napkins – the lovely soft rich marrow can be extracted with the handle of a teaspoon and is eaten on toast; it is also used as a flavouring (see Grilled Sirloin Steak with Beef Marrow and Shallots, page 61).

Melts   These are the spleen of an ox, calf or pig. Ox and calf's melts may be stuffed or used to make a stuffing themselves, as may pig's melts.

Sweetbreads   These are the two portions of the thymus gland – one in the throat and the other in the chest cavity (the heartbreads or pancreas) – of the calf and lamb. They are sold in pairs and considered a delicacy, especially the heartbreads from the calf. Lamb's sweetbreads are more common, but lack the delicacy of calf's. Prepare sweetbreads as for brains see page 45.

Tail   Oxtail is usually sold skinned and cut into segments. There is not a high proportion of meat to bone unless the tail is large and fat – thin tails may be cow tails and have less flavour. Good oxtail, with its proportion of connective tissue, cooked long and slow, makes a meltingly delicious stew with a round rich flavour. It is also good for soup.

Tongue   Ox tongue, available fresh and salted, has an excellent flavour. It can be boiled or braised and served hot with a sauce, or pressed and served sliced when cold. Lamb's tongue may be served in the same ways.

Tripe   This comes from all cud-chewing animals, but usually from three of the four stomachs of an ox. The first stomach is blanket (plain) tripe, the second honeycomb and the third thick seam. It is sold parboiled but requires further cooking – check with the butcher as to how long. It may be stewed or cooked in milk, or fried.

Fish

This chart is a seasonal guide to fresh seafish available in the British Isles. When shopping for fish, the indications of freshness are clear bright eyes, healthy pink to red gills, firm flesh and a sweet 'sea' smell. Any scales present should be firmly attached. Wherever possible, I prefer to buy a whole fish, rather than fillets or cutlets. A friendly fishmonger will be happy to prepare the fish to your requirements, and the head and trimmings may be used for making stock.

The groups and families of fish are versatile and interchangeable in recipes. Oily fish, like mackerel, herring, sardines and pilchards, are superb when simply grilled or barbecued. Many types of white fish, such as cod, hake, huss and haddock, have similar cooking characteristics and one may be substituted for another according to what is available.

Seasonal Fish Calendar

Fish	Jan	Feb	Mar	Apr	May	Jun	Jul	Aug	Sept	Oct	Nov	Dec
Anchovy						■	■	■	■	■	■	■
Bass	■	■	■			■		■	■	■	■	■
Bream	■	■	■			■	■	■	■	■	■	■
Brill	■	■				■	■	■	■	■	■	■
Carp	■	■	■			■	■	■	■	■	■	■
Char	■	■	■	■		■	■	■	■	■	■	■
Cockles	■	■	■	■	■	■	■	■	■	■		■
Cod	■	■	■	■	■			■	■	■	■	■
Coley	■	■				■	■	■	■	■	■	■
Crab	■	■	■	■	■	■	■	■	■	■	■	■
Crawfish	■	■	■	■	■	■	■	■	■	■	■	■
Crayfish	■	■	■	■		■	■	■	■	■	■	■
Dab	■	■	■	■	■			■	■	■	■	
Dover Sole	■	■				■	■	■	■	■	■	■
Dublin Bay Prawn	■	■	■	■	■	■	■	■	■	■	■	■
Eel	■	■	■	■	■	■	■	■	■	■	■	■
Flounder			■	■	■	■	■	■	■	■	■	
Grey Mullet	■	■	■			■	■	■	■	■	■	■
Haddock	■	■	■	■	■	■	■	■	■	■	■	■
Hake	■	■	■	■	■	■	■	■	■	■	■	■

Fish	Jan	Feb	Mar	Apr	May	Jun	Jul	Aug	Sept	Oct	Nov	Dec
Halibut						■	■	■	■	■	■	■
Herring	■	■				■	■	■	■	■	■	■
Huss	■	■	■	■	■	■	■	■	■	■	■	■
Lemon Sole	■	■	■		■	■	■	■	■	■	■	■
Lobster	■	■	■	■	■	■	■	■	■	■		■
Mackerel	■	■	■	■	■	■	■	■	■	■	■	■
Mussel									■	■	■	
Oyster	■	■	■	■					■	■	■	■
Pilchard	■	■		■		■	■	■	■	■	■	■
Plaice	■	■			■	■	■	■	■	■	■	■
Prawn	■	■	■	■	■	■	■	■	■	■		■
Red Mullet		■	■	■	■	■	■	■	■	■	■	■
Rainbow Trout	■	■	■	■	■	■	■	■	■	■	■	■
Salmon		■	■	■	■	■	■	■				
Scallop	■	■	■		■	■	■	■	■	■	■	■
Sea Bream	■	■	■			■	■	■	■	■	■	■
Shrimp	■	■	■	■	■	■	■	■	■	■	■	■
Skate	■	■			■	■	■	■	■	■	■	■
Sprat	■	■	■					■	■	■	■	■
Trout			■	■	■	■	■	■	■	■	■	■
Turbot	■	■			■	■	■	■	■	■	■	■
Whitebait		■	■	■	■	■			■	■	■	■
Whiting	■	■				■	■	■	■	■	■	■
Witch	■	■	■	■		■	■	■	■	■	■	■

■ = shaded areas indicate when fish is available

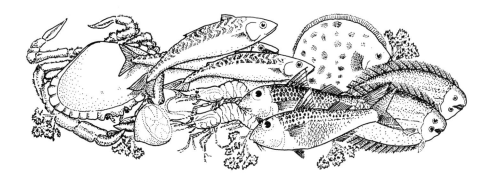

Vegetables

For the very best flavour, and in the ideal dream kitchen, vegetables are at their most delightful when picked or lifted from the garden just before they are to be prepared and cooked. This, however, is a joy only for those with enthusiasm, a well-planned garden, and that most valuable commodity . . . time.

The following chart is a seasonal guide to shopping for vegetables which will help you to buy vegetables when they should be at their best. Remember that the price, appearance and packaging of vegetables is not always an indication of their quality and flavour. This may be as true for wrinkled-up, badly packaged and transported 'organic' produce, as it may be for smart, uniform and tasteless imported vegetables.

Store vegetables in a cool dark larder or in the crisper drawer of your refrigerator. Green leaf vegetables should be eaten as soon as possible as their vitamin content soon dwindles.

Seasonal Vegetable Calendar

Vegetables	Jan	Feb	Mar	Apr	May	Jun	Jul	Aug	Sept	Oct	Nov	Dec
Asparagus					▓	▓						
Aubergines							▓	▓	▓			
Beans, broad					▓	▓	▓	▓				
Beans, French						▓	▓	▓	▓			
Beans, runner							▓	▓	▓	▓		
Beetroot						▓	▓	▓	▓			
Broccoli			▓	▓								
Brussels sprouts	▓										▓	▓
Cabbages	▓			▓	▓				▓	▓		
Carrots					▓	▓	▓	▓				
Cauliflowers	▓	▓	▓	▓						▓	▓	▓
Celeriac									▓	▓	▓	▓
Celery	▓	▓						▓	▓	▓	▓	▓
Courgettes							▓	▓	▓	▓		
Fennel								▓	▓			
Leeks	▓	▓									▓	▓
Lettuce						▓	▓	▓				
Marrows							▓	▓	▓	▓		
Mushrooms	▓	▓	▓	▓	▓	▓	▓	▓	▓	▓	▓	▓
Onions								▓	▓	▓	▓	▓
Parsnips	▓	▓								▓	▓	▓
Peas						▓	▓	▓				
Peppers							▓	▓	▓			
Potatoes						▓	▓	▓				
Spinach	▓	▓	▓	▓				▓	▓	▓	▓	▓
Swedes	▓	▓						▓	▓	▓	▓	▓
Sweetcorn								▓	▓	▓		
Tomatoes							▓	▓	▓	▓		
Turnips	▓	▓	▓					▓	▓	▓	▓	▓

▓ = shaded areas indicate when vegetables are at their best

Beef

Traditional roast beef and Yorkshire pudding

Although there are many approaches to producing the definitive dinner of roast beef with Yorkshire pudding, beautiful gravy and horseradish sauce, I am sure all cooks would agree that the most vital ingredient is perfect timing! *I hope that the following discourse does not make a very simple roast seem complicated. But because such a roast, for which you will be using the best meat and ingredients available, is nowadays an expensive and therefore occasional dinner, I think it is worth some consideration – especially if you are cooking it for the first time.*

The pudding or puddings can be served first, with a little of the juices or blood from the meat, but I prefer to serve them with the beef. I was brought up on these traditional roasts, and my father, a Yorkshireman who knows his meat, was the carver and always made the puddings too. So obviously I think our method is one of the best; and with good-quality meat we certainly don't go in for rubbing it with mustard or flour or herbs and spices. We also prefer individual puddings to one large one so that everyone gets a fair deal with crispy puffed-up rims and soft centres.

However, for my method of timing, I have the advantage of cooking either in my Aga or in my electric double oven. The extra just-warm oven gives me the necessary room for keeping things warm and ready, and allowing the meat to relax, while I finish off the puddings in the hot oven and the gravy on top of the stove. If you don't have two ovens, or enough room on the top of the stove to create a 'keeping-warm' area, I suggest you resign yourself to less-than-perfect Yorkshire puddings as you will have to cook them earlier in the timing sequence.

The other important part of this meal is the gravy. Some people – especially the French – prefer the pan juices, perhaps reduced, with a little vegetable stock added and reduced again. Others – especially the English – prefer a gravy thickened with flour. Depending on the time available and my mood, I like both ways. But it's important to make sure when preparing the roux *(for thickening) that the flour is really 'cooked out' (see page 16), and in this recipe I give both methods in their correct sequence.*

I used Galloway beef last time I cooked a roast, a Scottish breed like the Angus which produces beautiful flavoursome meat. Forerib (on the bone) is my favourite joint for roasting. It is not worth roasting a piece of less than 4–5 lb (1.8–2.3 kg): smaller pieces, whatever the cut, will shrink and are often dry and tough. Remember to choose well-hung beef from a good butcher (see page 18 for information on shopping for meat).

Adjust the amount of potatoes and vegetables to the number of people you are serving and to their appetites.

Serves at least 6

About 1½ lb (700 g) potatoes, peeled

1 large onion, peeled and quartered

Salt

1 lb (450 g) parsnips, peeled (optional)

4–5 lb (1.8–2.3 kg) forerib of beef

Freshly ground black pepper

A little oil

1 tablespoon flour (optional)

Yorkshire Pudding Batter:

4 oz (110 g) white flour

Pinch of salt

1 egg

5 fl oz (150 ml) milk

5 fl oz (150 ml) water

To serve:

Carrots and/or Brussels sprouts

Horseradish sauce

Pre-heat the oven to gas mark 8, 450°F (230°C).

In a basin whisk together the Yorkshire pudding ingredients until absolutely smooth, then pour into a jug and set aside in a cool place.

Put the potatoes and the onion in a pan of lightly salted boiling water and simmer for about 10 minutes, depending on size, to part-cook. Do the same with the parsnips (if using) in a separate pan. Drain, discarding the onion (which is for flavour only) and saving the cooking water. Set aside.

Meanwhile, wipe the joint with dampened kitchen paper and pat dry. Set it on a rack or trivet over a deep roasting tin, season with salt and pepper and drizzle over a little oil. Put into the oven and roast for 15–20 minutes. Take the beef out of the oven and very quickly arrange the potatoes and parsnips (if using) in the bottom of the roasting tin, turn them in the dripping and replace the beef on its rack over the vegetables. Return the roasting tin to the oven and turn the heat down to gas mark 4, 350°F (180°C). The vegetables will now roast beautifully with the fatty juices from the beef dripping down over them. Continue to cook the beef over the vegetables for a further hour or so, depending on how rare you like your beef to be. Strictly speaking to be 'correctly' roasted, beef should be slightly underdone: delicately pink inside with a deep brown crisp exterior. Those at the table who prefer their beef well done can take the first slice or two from the outside of the joint. Cooking a joint of beef to 'well done' will usually result in dryness.

Towards the end of the cooking time, prepare and cook the carrots and/or Brussels sprouts. Drain them, saving the cooking water, and keep them warm in a warmed serving dish covered with buttered greaseproof paper and a lid. (For better results, however, if you are a very quick and confident worker and can cope with gravy making, carving and six other things at the same time, you can leave the cooking of the vegetables until the very last moment before serving.)

When the beef is cooked, lift it on to a hot plate and leave it to rest for 15 minutes in a warm place. Use a slotted spoon to transfer the roast potatoes and parsnips to another warmed serving dish and keep these warm too. Turn the oven up to gas mark 6, 400°F (200°C).

If you intend to make a thick gravy, pour 1 tablespoon of the dripping from the roasting tin into a small saucepan and set aside. Then pour just a little more of the dripping from the roasting tin into individual Yorkshire pudding tins. Set the roasting tin and its remaining juices aside. Put the pudding tins into the hot oven and leave for 2 minutes or until the dripping is hot and smoking, then quickly pour a little batter into each one and return them to the oven. Cook the puddings for 15–20 minutes or until well risen.

Meanwhile, prepare the gravy. Set the roasting tin with its remaining juices on the top of the stove, add a cup of the reserved vegetable cooking water and heat. Stir well, scraping all the juices off the bottom of the tin. Boil hard, stirring all the time, then add more vegetable water and boil hard again to reduce and thicken slightly. This produces a nice tasty gravy which may need straining if there are scraps of roast potato and parsnip floating around in it. If you wish to make a thicker gravy, add 1 tablespoon flour to the reserved dripping in the saucepan and cook over a gentle heat, stirring until the flour is slightly brown and well blended with the fat to form a *roux*. Gradually add the prepared gravy to the *roux* and continue to cook, stirring all the time, until the desired smoothness and thickness is achieved – add more vegetable water if necessary.

While the joint has been resting, delicious juices will have seeped out of it; carefully pour these into the gravy, and transfer it to a warmed jug. Carve the meat at the table, which is by now laden with the hot covered dishes of potatoes and other vegetables, the jug of gravy and a bowl of horseradish sauce. Just as the warmed plates of meat are being passed around and everyone is serving themselves to vegetables, fly back to the oven and take out the Yorkshire puddings which should by now be cooked beautifully – this is the very best time to serve them, straight from the oven when they are puffed up and perfect.

Beef with prunes

Here is a simple adaptation of a French recipe for left-over cooked beef, in which you can use left-over brisket from the preceding recipe. It makes an extremely quick and tasty family main course and is good served with plain noodles and perhaps some braised cabbage.

Serves 4

8 oz (225 g) prunes, stoned

About 10 fl oz (300 ml) red wine

2 tablespoons olive oil

3–4 large onions, peeled and finely sliced

Pinch of salt

Freshly ground black pepper

A little beef stock (optional)

½ tablespoon tarragon vinegar or white wine vinegar (or to taste)

12 oz–1 lb (350–450 g) cold cooked salt brisket of beef (see page 59), thinly sliced and trimmed of fat

First simmer the prunes in the red wine for 10 minutes. Meanwhile, heat the oil in a large frying-pan or wok (particularly useful for this dish). Very gently fry the onions in the oil over a low heat, seasoning them with just a pinch of salt and lots of freshly ground pepper. Continue cooking them for about 15–20 minutes or until they are totally soft and cooked right down, but do not allow them to brown. Then tip in the wine and prunes, adding a little more wine or some stock if there does not seem to be enough liquid. Add ½ tablespoon tarragon vinegar or wine vinegar. Now put in the slices of brisket and gently turn them once into the onions. Cover the pan and cook at scarcely simmering for about 10 minutes. Taste to see if you need to add a little more vinegar before serving.

Sauerbraten (marinated beef pot roast)

My appetite breathtakingly whetted by the local schnapps, I enjoyed the fabulous flavour of this German dish for the first time one memorable evening in a beautiful old Westphalian country cottage, where it was served with precise authenticity. It's a very easy recipe, but you need to start the preparation 3–5 days in advance because the meat needs that long to marinate. It is the marinade that makes the meat so very tender and succulent and forms the basis of a delicious sweet and sour gravy. Serve with home-made noodles and apple sauce, or braised red cabbage and dumplings.

Serves 6–8

4–5 lb (1.8–2.3 kg) piece topside of beef

A little oil for frying

1 carrot, peeled and sliced

1 medium onion, peeled and sliced

4 sticks celery, sliced

1 leek, trimmed and sliced

1 handful raisins

3 oz (75 g) German honey cake or gingersnaps, crumbled

Pinch of salt

Freshly ground black pepper

A little lemon juice or wine vinegar (optional)

Marinade:

7 fl oz (200 ml) red wine

7 fl oz (200 ml) red wine vinegar

1 large onion, peeled and sliced

2–3 bay leaves, broken in half

1–2 sticks celery, sliced

1 teaspoon crushed black peppercorns

1 teaspoon crushed juniper berries

½ teaspoon crushed cloves

Trim the beef of all fat and, if necessary, tie with kitchen string so that it does not fall apart in the final cooking. Quickly rinse the joint under running water and pat dry with kitchen paper. Put the meat into an earthenware or glass bowl into which it fits quite snugly.

In a large saucepan bring the marinade ingredients to the boil and simmer for just 2 minutes. Strain the marinade over the beef. Cover the beef and leave it in a cool place for 3–5 days, depending on the warmth and humidity of the weather. You can put it in the refrigerator if you do not have a cool larder – in which case it can be left for the maximum time. Turn the beef 2 or 3 times each day.

When you are ready to cook, pre-heat the oven to gas mark 3, 325°F (170°C). Lift the meat out of the marinade and pat it dry with kitchen paper. Reserve the marinade. In a large heavy frying-pan heat a little oil and brown the meat in it on all sides. Transfer to a flameproof casserole. Now gently fry the vegetables in the frying-pan and, using a slotted spoon, add them to the beef. Pour a little of the marinade into the frying-pan and heat, scraping up all the juices from the bottom of the pan; add this and the remaining marinade to the casserole. Don't add salt at this stage. Very slowly and gently bring the casserole up to simmering point, then cover tightly with a double thickness of aluminium foil and a lid. Put the casserole in the oven and cook for 2½–3 hours or until the meat is tender.

Transfer the cooked beef to a warmed serving dish and keep it warm. Now strain the cooking liquid into a saucepan and boil hard to reduce it somewhat, and add the raisins and crumbled honey cake or gingersnaps to flavour and thicken it. Taste, season with a little salt and pepper and add a squeeze of lemon juice or wine vinegar if you think it is too sweet. Slice the beef and arrange it on the serving dish. Hand the gravy separately in a jug.

Salt brisket

'Salt beef on rye' sandwiches have become very popular in city sandwich bars. The cut used is silverside, but I wondered how they would taste made with brisket – one of my favourite cheaper cuts of meat. I therefore found a butcher selling salt brisket; I used fresh granary bread as I couldn't find any rye, and filled the sandwiches (unbuttered, of course) very generously with thick slices of the hot brisket. Served with pickled cucumber, they were truly delicious.

To cook brisket, whether salted or unsalted, buy a large piece weighing about 5 lb (2.3 kg) – smaller pieces tend to shrink and often there is too much fat in proportion to the lean meat. This will provide at least two meals and some good stock. Before cooking, salt brisket, which will have been brined for about a week, may need soaking in water for 2 hours or so, but check with the butcher who will be happy to advise you.

Any left-over cooked brisket may be used in made-up dishes: for instance, in a cottage pie served with gravy made from the reduced stock; or it may be served sliced and carefully re-heated or cold with a devil sauce; or chopped finely or minced and mixed with creamed potatoes, softened onions, horseradish and herbs and baked in the oven; or used in Beef with Prunes (see page 57).

Serves 6

5 lb (2.3 kg) piece salt brisket of beef

1 onion, peeled, quartered and stuck with cloves

2–3 carrots, peeled and roughly chopped

12 black peppercorns, crushed

1 bay leaf

A few sprigs parsley

Pre-heat the oven to gas mark 1, 275°F (140°C). Place the meat in a flameproof casserole – it should be quite a snug fit. Add the onion, carrots, crushed peppercorns, bay leaf and parsley. Cover with water. Heat on top of the stove until scarcely simmering, cover tightly, and transfer to the oven to cook for about 5 hours or until the meat is very tender.

To serve hot, lift the meat out of the cooking liquid, let it rest for a few minutes and slice thickly. To serve cold, place the drained meat in a dish with a weighted plate on top to press, allow to cool, then refrigerate for several hours before slicing thinly. Strain the stock and leave it to cool overnight. On the following day remove the hard crust of fat from the surface, strain the clear stock again and reserve it for use in another recipe.

Grilled sirloin steak with beef marrow and shallots

This is my highly anglicised adaptation of entrecôte à la Bordelaise – *the speciality of Bordeaux. Because most home cooks will have difficulty in feeding their domestic barbecues with 'burned old wood from chestnut wine barrels and vine cuttings', I decided that the steak must be nearly as wonderful cooked* under *the grill as it undoubtedly is when cooked over the fire. Not only that; I then decided that the steaks should be served on squares of crisp herbed Yorkshire pudding, with minted puréed peas and a potato gratin. This eclectic approach resulted in an excellent and memorable main course.*

If you don't like the idea of sawing up a marrow bone yourself, ask your butcher to do it.

Serves 4

1 quantity Yorkshire Pudding Batter (see page 55)

1 tablespoon chopped fresh herbs (parsley, thyme, etc.) or ½–1 teaspoon mixed dried herbs

4 sirloin steaks, 1½–2 inches (3–5 cm) thick

Pinch of salt

Freshly ground black pepper

A little olive oil

1 beef marrow bone, sawn into 2–3 inch (5–7.5 cm) pieces

1 good handful parsley, very finely chopped

8 oz (225 g) shallots, peeled and very finely chopped

Make the Yorkshire Pudding Batter at least 1 hour in advance, add the herbs and leave to rest.

Trim the steaks of all visible fat, wipe with dampened kitchen paper and pat dry. Season lightly with salt and pepper, brush with a little olive oil and set aside. The steaks should be at room temperature before grilling.

Rinse the pieces of marrow bone in cold water, then simmer them in a large pan of water for 20 minutes. Strain. With the handle of a teaspoon prise the pinkish-grey marrow out of the bone pieces.

When you are ready to cook, pre-heat the oven to gas mark 6, 400°F (200°C). Heat a little olive oil in a roasting tin in the oven until it is sizzling. Pour in just enough batter to cover the base of the tin – too much and you will have a thick soggy pudding – and cook in the oven for about 20 minutes or until risen and golden-brown.

Meanwhile, pre-heat the grill until it is good and hot. Oil the grill rack. After the Yorkshire pudding has been cooking for 10 minutes, grill the steaks for 3 minutes on each side (for rare to medium rare). Take the grill pan away from the heat and, using a knife, spread the marrow over the top of the steaks, sprinkle with a little parsley and all of the shallots. Take the Yorkshire pudding from the oven, cut it into 4 equal pieces and divide between 4 warmed plates. Flash the steaks under the hot grill for 30 seconds, then set each one on its pudding: the meat and marrow juices run deliciously into the pudding. Serve immediately, garnished with the remaining parsley.

Fillets of steak with mushroom pâté en croûte

This is one of my versions of the expensive, rich and entertaining dish of boeuf en croûte. *Filo pastry is lighter than the customary puff or flaky pastry, and because it uses individual steaks the recipe is obviously less costly than if it called for a whole fillet. The quantities can be easily adjusted to serve two, three or more guests.*

The mushroom pâté is very versatile: as well as in this dish you can use it for enriching basic soups, as a stuffing for rolled joints of meat, for enlivening gravies and sauces, to fill omelettes and pancakes, with pasta, or spread on crackers or fingers of toast. It will keep in the refrigerator for several days.

Serve Fillets of Steak with Mushroom Pâté en Croûte with baby carrots, spinach and tiny cauliflower florets.

Serves 4

4 fillet steaks about 1½ inches (3 cm) thick

Pinch of salt

Freshly ground black pepper

1 tablespoon brandy

Sunflower oil

8 sheets filo pastry (see page 16), thawed if frozen

1 tablespoon finely chopped parsley

1 egg, beaten

Mushroom Pâté:

½ large onion, peeled and coarsely chopped

1–2 cloves garlic, peeled and coarsely chopped

12 oz (350 g) mushrooms, wiped and halved or quartered, including the stems

15 fl oz (400 ml) red wine

2 oz (50 g) butter

Pinch of salt

Freshly ground black pepper

First make the pâté. Put the onion and garlic into the bowl of a food processor or liquidiser and whizz on high speed for a few seconds until finely chopped. Now add the mushrooms and wine and whizz again in short bursts until the mushrooms are very finely chopped. Put this mixture into a heavy saucepan, bring gently to the boil, then turn down the heat and simmer, uncovered, for about 30–45 minutes or until the liquid has nearly vanished and the mixture is a concentrated paste. Stir in the butter, season with salt and pepper and turn into a dish to cool.

Pre-heat the oven to gas mark 6, 400°F (200°C). When you are ready to cook, trim the fillet steaks of visible fat, wipe with dampened kitchen paper and pat dry. Season very lightly with salt and pepper and brush with brandy. Heat a large heavy frying-pan, add 1–2 tablespoons sunflower oil and, when it is very hot, sear the steaks in it for about 15 seconds on each side. Remove and set aside on a plate to cool.

Calculate the size of pastry you will need to parcel each steak and cut out 16 rectangles or squares: you will use 4 for each parcel. Brush 1 square very lightly with sunflower oil, place another square on top, brush again and repeat with 2 more squares; these will form the first parcel. Spread a little of the pâté on the centre of the pastry, scatter with a little of the parsley and place a steak on top. Scatter with more parsley and top with more of the pâté. Fold the edges up and over to make a parcel, brushing with a little more oil to seal. Turn the parcel over and place it on a lightly oiled baking sheet. Continue in the same way until you have made 4 parcels, brush them all with a little beaten egg and bake in the oven for 15–20 minutes – this will result in the steaks being pink on the inside.

If you would like a quickly made sauce to serve with this dish, fry the steaks in 1 oz (25 g) butter instead of oil. When you have removed the steaks, add a little red wine to the hot pan to de-glaze, then add 1–2 tablespoons of the mushroom pâté together with about 4 tablespoons good meat stock or more red wine. Cook until heated through, strain and check the seasoning. Add about 2 tablespoons cream or a nut of butter to finish. Keep warm or gently re-heat to serve.

Beef in beer

This is an adaptation of carbonnade of beef, a delicious dark Flemish stew which is traditionally served with bread and mustard. If possible, start by cooking the meat a day in advance. Serve with potatoes and steamed greens or a crisp salad.

Serves 4

2 lb (900 g) stewing steak

About 15 fl oz (400 ml) brown or pale ale

1 bouquet garni

Pinch of salt

Freshly ground black pepper

2 tablespoons olive oil

2 onions, peeled and chopped

2 fat cloves garlic, peeled and crushed

1 heaped tablespoon flour

Dash of vinegar (optional)

Dijon mustard to taste

1 French stick, sliced

The day before – or at least several hours before – you intend to eat, pre-heat the oven to gas mark 2, 300°F (150°C).

Trim the beef of all visible fat and cut it into largish neat pieces. Lay them in a heavy flameproof casserole, add the beer and top up with a little water if necessary to cover. Put in the bouquet garni and season with salt and pepper. Heat very gently on top of the stove until barely simmering, then cover tightly with a double thickness of aluminium foil and the lid. Put the casserole in the oven and cook without disturbing for 3 hours. Carefully transfer the stew to a basin, cool, cover and refrigerate.

The following day remove the fat from the surface of the stew by first skimming then blotting with absorbent kitchen paper. Heat the olive oil in the casserole and gently fry the onions in it until they are totally soft but not brown, adding the garlic for the final minute of frying. Stir in the flour and cook gently for 1–2 minutes, then remove from the heat and stir in some of the stock until well amalgamated. Carefully put all the meat and remaining stock back into the casserole. Very slowly and gently re-heat on top of the stove until just simmering. Check the seasoning, adjusting if necessary, and add a dash of vinegar if you wish. Continue to cook gently for 30 minutes.

Roast saddle of Welsh lamb (page 88), and Braised celery and chestnuts with creamy cheese sauce (page 193)

You may need to add a little more water if the stew is too thick and reduced.

Spread the Dijon mustard on the slices of French bread. These can be pushed, mustard side up, into the top of the stew to soak up a little gravy, then browned for 15 minutes under a medium grill. Alternatively, serve the bread separately at the table with the potatoes and accompanying vegetables suggested above.

Grilled spiced steak kebabs

You really do need quite tender beef for these kebabs – but a little fillet steak goes a long way. The aroma and taste is unbelievably sweet and fragrant. Serve with a herbed or spiced pilaff and a crisp green salad; or, for a summer barbecue, cradle the kebabs in split salad-filled baguettes or sections of French loaf and drizzle over a little of the marinade.

Serves 4

2–3 fillet steaks, cut into 1–1½ inch (2.5–3 cm) cubes

About 20 cherry tomatoes or 1 red and 1 green pepper, de-seeded and cut into 1–1½ inch (2.5–3 cm) squares

A little oil for greasing

Marinade:

6 tablespoons olive oil

4 tablespoons fresh orange juice

4 cloves garlic, peeled and very finely chopped

About 1 teaspoon cayenne pepper

1 teaspoon ground cumin

6 cardamom pods, broken

Pinch of salt

Freshly ground black pepper

Combine the marinade ingredients in an earthenware or glass bowl, add the cubes of meat and toss to coat thoroughly. Leave to marinate for 2 hours.

Thread the steak cubes on to oiled skewers, alternating them with whole cherry tomatoes or squares of pepper.

When you are ready to cook, pre-heat the grill and get it good and hot. Oil the grill rack. Cook the kebabs under the grill, basting them occasionally with the marinade. Serve immediately.

Tropical chicken with lime and rum (page 134), Minty lamb in filo packages (page 93), and Chilli pork and spinach stir-fry (page 111)

Beef olives

A variation of an old favourite – lean, tender, economical and low in fat. I like to serve these olives with pasta and steamed broccoli.

Serves 4–6

1 lb (450 g) piece lean topside of beef or braising steak

1–2 tablespoons good-quality olive oil

A little yoghurt or thin cream and sprigs of coriander to garnish

Stuffing:

6–8 oz (175–225 g) wholewheat breadcrumbs

Grated rind and juice of ½ lemon

1 small onion, peeled and very finely chopped

1 tablespoon finely chopped fresh coriander or 1–2 teaspoons ground coriander

Pinch of salt

Freshly ground black pepper

1 egg, beaten, to bind

Sauce:

1 × 14 oz (400 g) tin tomatoes, puréed, or 1 × 14 oz (400 g) carton *passata*

5–10 fl oz (150–300 ml) stock

10 fl oz (300 ml) red wine

First thoroughly chill the meat in the refrigerator or put it in the freezer and leave for 30 minutes: this makes it easier to slice thinly.

Meanwhile, combine the stuffing ingredients. You should have a fairly moist yet firm mixture – add a drop more lemon juice if necessary.

Now cut the chilled beef into very thin slices measuring about 3 × 3 inches (7.5 × 7.5 cm) or 2 × 3 inches (5 × 7.5 cm) according to the shape and size of your piece of meat. Trim off any visible fat as you go. Spread the stuffing on the slices of beef and roll them up, fastening each one with a wooden cocktail stick or tying it with kitchen string. (You can prepare the dish up to this point a day or a few hours in advance if you wish.)

When you are ready to cook, pre-heat the oven to gas mark 3, 325°F (170°C). Heat the olive oil in a large heavy frying-pan and gently brown the 'olives' in it. Drain them on kitchen paper before packing them into a casserole. Combine the sauce ingredients and stir them into the meaty juices in the frying-pan. Heat to boiling point and pour over the meat, if necessary adding a little more wine or stock so that the olives are completely covered. Put on the lid (or a double thickness of aluminium foil) and cook in the oven for about 1–1½ hours.

To serve, lift out the olives with a slotted spoon and remove the sticks or string. Arrange them in rows or in a circle (with pasta if that is what you have chosen as an accompaniment) on a warmed serving dish and keep warm. Pour the sauce into a heavy saucepan and boil hard to reduce it somewhat. Then pour it all over the arranged olives, swirl a trickle of yoghurt or thin cream over and garnish with sprigs of coriander.

Special domed individual steak and mushroom pie

This adaptation of Sussex pond stew has a complex and intense flavour, and yet takes very little preparation or skill. I like it with mashed potatoes and no-nonsense carrots.

Serves 4

1½ lb (700 g) good-quality chuck, skirt or top rump steak

1–2 tablespoons seasoned flour

1 large onion, peeled and sliced into rings

1 bottle stout (preferably Guinness)

1 glass port

Salt

Freshly ground black pepper

8 oz (225 g) mushrooms, wiped

1 lb (450 g) puff pastry, thawed if frozen

1 egg yolk, beaten, to glaze

Pre-heat the oven to gas mark 3, 325°F (170°C).

Trim the meat of all visible fat and cut it into 2 × 1 inch (5 × 2.5 cm) pieces. Put it with the seasoned flour into a paper or polythene bag and shake until all the meat is lightly coated.

Pack the meat in one layer in the bottom of a large, heavy, flameproof casserole, cover with the onion rings and pour in the stout and port. Cover the dish very tightly with a double thickness of aluminium foil and a lid. Bring to simmering point on the top of the stove, then put into the oven and cook for about 2 hours. Check the meat after this time, add salt and pepper to taste, then scatter in the mushrooms and continue cooking for another 30 minutes. Cool the stew and remove any solidified fat. (You can prepare the dish up to this point a day or two in advance if you wish: this is typical of the kind of stew that improves on re-heating.)

On a cool floured surface roll out the pastry very thinly and leave it to relax for 30 minutes. Have ready 4 shallow ramekins, ovenproof soup bowls or tureens *without* lips or rims in which to make the pies. Using a tea plate, cut 4 rounds of pastry of a size which will allow a 1 inch (2.5 cm) overlap when placed on the pie dishes. Divide the steak, onions, mushrooms and their delicious dark liquid between the dishes. Paint beaten egg yolk in a ½ inch (1 cm) wide border around the edge of the pastry circles and place one over each of the pie dishes. Cup your hands around the edge to press down and entirely seal the pastry. (Because it is the steam produced during cooking that causes the pastry to dome, the lid must be totally air-tight so that no steam can escape.) Put the pies in the refrigerator for at least 1 hour – several hours won't hurt.

When you are ready to cook, pre-heat the oven to gas mark 6, 400°F (200°C). Brush the pastry with egg yolk and bake for 10–15 minutes or until the pie lids are well domed and golden. Now turn the oven down to gas mark 4, 350°F (180°C), and continue to cook for a further 15 minutes or so to allow the meat to re-heat thoroughly. Serve immediately – your guests burst into their pies using spoons and forks!

Shin of beef stewed with herbed dumplings

An inexpensive, nourishing, old-fashioned, family stew topped with golden crusty suet dumplings – no wine or 'fancy' ingredients are included, just the honest flavours of good-quality meat and vegetables, carefully cooked and often secretly more appreciated by sophisticates than is widely acknowledged. Every family member from babies to grandparents loves this kind of stew. I am particularly fond of the dumplings because, iceberg-like, two thirds of each one hide in the gravy, absorbing its comforting taste. Vegetable suet can be used with the same results and, if you like, you can flavour them with a mixture of parsley and thyme or parsley and sage instead of parsley alone.

Serves 6–8

3 lb (1.4 kg) shin of beef

1 large onion, peeled and chopped

1–2 carrots, peeled and chopped

1 turnip or piece swede, peeled and chopped

Pinch of salt

Freshly ground black pepper

1 bunch herbs (bay leaf, parsley, thyme)

2–3 lamb's kidneys, cored and sliced (optional)

Dumplings:

6 oz (175 g) self-raising flour

3 oz (75 g) suet

1 tablespoon finely chopped parsley

Pinch of salt

Freshly ground black pepper

Put the beef in one piece into a deep heavy saucepan or flameproof casserole. Add all the vegetables, seasoning and herbs, cover with cold water and slowly bring to the boil. Skim if necessary, cover and simmer for 3 hours. This could be done in a very low oven if you prefer – say, gas mark 2, 300°F (150°C) – but you must make sure that the liquid never boils.

By now the beef should be just tender – *not* all ragged and cooked to shreds. Carefully transfer it to a plate along with the vegetables and quickly cool the stock (see page 12). Using first a spoon, then absorbent kitchen paper, skim and blot off all the fat that has risen to the surface. Return the de-greased stock to the saucepan or casserole and boil fiercely to reduce it to about 15 fl oz (400 ml). Mash or process the vegetables to a fine purée, then return to the pan of stock. Slice the beef neatly and return it to the stock. The stew may be prepared up to this point a day in advance if you wish.

When you are ready to finish the stew, pre-heat the oven to gas mark 5, 375°F (190°C). If you are using kidneys, add these now.

To make the dumplings, combine the flour, suet, parsley, salt and pepper and, using a knife, quickly draw in a little cold water to form a soft but not sticky dough. Handling the dough as little as possible, form it into 6–8 small dumplings. Settle these into the top of the stew and cook in the oven for approximately 40 minutes or until the dumplings have a golden crust, the stew is thoroughly heated through and the kidneys are cooked.

Spicy meatballs with pasta

An economical dish for which you could use lean minced lamb instead of beef. Adjust the spices to your preference.

Serves 4

1 lb (450 g) lean chuck steak, minced, or best-quality minced beef

1 onion, peeled and very finely chopped or grated

1 fat clove garlic, peeled and chopped

Pinch of salt

Freshly ground black pepper

½–1 teaspoon ground coriander

½ teaspoon ground cumin

2 teaspoons garam masala

2–3 oz (50–75 g) breadcrumbs

1 egg, lightly beaten

1 tablespoon flour

Sunflower oil for frying

1 quantity Fresh Tomato Sauce (see page 214)

Grated cheese (optional)

About 1 lb (450 g) pasta shapes, cooked, to serve

If the meat is not already minced, trim it of all visible fat and either pass it through a mincer or process it fairly finely in a food processor. Alternatively, ask your butcher to mince it for you. In a large bowl mix together the meat, onion, garlic, seasoning, spices and breadcrumbs, kneading and squeezing well to distribute the spices thoroughly. Bind with the egg, shape into small meatballs and dredge lightly with flour. Chill for 1–2 hours.

When you are ready to cook, pre-heat the oven to gas mark 4, 350°F (180°C). Heat a little oil in a frying-pan or wok and brown the meatballs in it on all sides. Drain them well on kitchen paper. Place them in a shallow baking dish and pour over the Fresh Tomato Sauce. Bake in the oven for about 30 minutes. The dish can easily be kept warm for a while in a low oven and served with the pasta when you are ready to eat. You can sprinkle the meatballs with grated cheese and brown under the grill before serving if you wish.

A beef curry

Although I enjoy and prefer to use a variety of separate spices for authentic Indian dishes, I do sometimes resort to this very quickly prepared curry. Obviously not as singular and subtle as the various classic curried dishes, this recipe produces a delicious stew which should be served with immaculately cooked plain rice and various chutneys.

Use good-quality curry powder, adding 2–3 tablespoons according to your taste, and bear in mind that, as with many casseroles and stews, this dish is even better when cooked the day before and re-heated – store it in the refrigerator in an earthenware or glass bowl.

Serves 4–6

1½ lb (700 g) chuck steak

2 large onions

4 tablespoons sunflower oil

2–3 fat cloves garlic, peeled and crushed

2–3 tablespoons good-quality curry powder

½ teaspoon chilli powder

15 fl oz (400 ml) stock or water

1 tablespoon mango chutney (including a large piece of mango, finely chopped)

2 apples, cored and cut into large pieces (leave skin on)

1 teaspoon brown sugar

Juice of ½ lemon

Freshly ground black pepper

Pre-heat the oven to gas mark 3, 325°F (170°C).

Trim and cube the meat. Peel the onions and slice into rings; cut the rings in half to form crescents. In a large, heavy, flameproof casserole heat the oil and add the onions and garlic. Add the curry powder and chilli powder at the same time and fry gently for 10 minutes or until the onions are soft and golden. Add the meat and brown, stirring all the time. Now add the stock or water, bring to simmering point and add the chutney, apples sugar and lemon juice. Season with black pepper. Cover and cook in the oven for 2–3 hours. If necessary, reduce the curry sauce on top of the stove before serving.

Cornish pasty

A proper home-made Cornish pasty, wrapped in a napkin and eaten in the hand is the original complete convenience main course. Unfortunately, its reputation has suffered from the mass-produced travesties. Here's how it should be done: a small amount of best lean chuck steak or skirt should be cut into very small pieces and combined with neat slices of potato, onion and swede or turnip, seasoned with salt and pepper and cooked in shortcrust pastry. That's it, plain and simple – no fatty minced meat, no peas or carrots, garlic, herbs or gravy. The true Cornish pasty is a simple yet succulent marriage of honest flavours with no fuss. Every day during the season Julia Parkhouse makes a batch of the best-ever pasties for the pub on the island where I live, but to avoid disappointment you must book one or queue or have an argument – or make your own following her recipe, which is given below. Once you have made the pastry and prepared the vegetables, you might as well make a good batch, because they do freeze well.

Makes 6 pasties

1 lb (450 g) lean skirt or chuck steak, trimmed and cut into small pieces

4 oz (110 g) onion, peeled and chopped

8 oz (225 g) potato, peeled and cut into small neat pieces

6 oz (175 g) swede, peeled and cut into small cubes

Pinch of salt

Freshly ground black pepper

1 egg, beaten

Shortcrust pastry:

12 oz (350 g) plain white flour

Pinch salt

3 oz (75 g) chilled butter, diced

3 oz (75 g) White Flora (sunflower oil and blended vegetable oil fat) or equivalent, diced

Chilled water to mix

Make the pastry a good hour or so in advance – better still the day before. Sift the flour and salt into a cool mixing bowl. Hold the sieve high above the bowl so that you incorporate as much air as possible. Add the diced butter and Flora. Use cool fingers and a light touch to rub the fat into the flour, lifting your hands high so that you keep the pastry light and aerated. Do not overdo the rubbing in. Shake the mixing bowl now and then to bring large lumps of fat to the surface. When the mixture resembles fine breadcrumbs, use a cold palette knife or ordinary knife to mix in just enough chilled water to form a ball of pastry with a nice short consistency. Do not handle it too much or knead it. Wrap or cover the pastry in foil or greaseproof paper, and rest it in the refrigerator, for at least 30 minutes before using

When you are ready to cook, pre-heat the oven to gas mark 6, 400°F (200°C). Put all the meat, onion, potato and swede into large mixing bowl, season well with salt and pepper and combine thoroughly. Cut a wedge of pastry and roll it out on a floured board. Using a salad plate (the size between dinner and side plate) cut out a round of pastry. Heap about one sixth of the meat and vegetable mixture into the centre of the round: the secret of the pasty is that it must be full to bursting at the start; otherwise when it is cooked you will have a half-hollow pasty. Brush the rim of the pastry circle with water or beaten egg and bring the edges up to the centre to join, teasing in any filling that tries to escape. Crimp the seal, then gently push down and away from you so that the pastry settles. Make the other five pasties in the same way.

Transfer the pasties to a floured baking sheet, brush them with beaten egg and bake in the oven for 20 minutes. Then turn down the oven to gas mark 4, 350°F (180°C) and continue baking for a further 40 minutes. After removing the pasties from the oven, let them rest for 5 minutes before wrapping them in paper napkins to serve. Hand salt, pepper and mustard or Worcestershire sauce separately if desired.

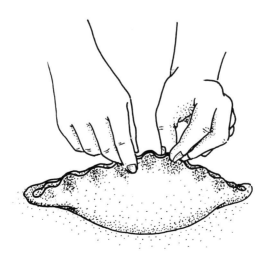

Pasta with bolognese sauce

Too often this classic sauce is regarded as sort of beginner's quick bed-sit kind of dish: any old butcher's fatty minced beef is hurled into a pan with a tin of tomatoes, various herbs and rough red wine, and cooked through in less than 30 minutes. This approach results in a crude and gritty sauce, far removed from the smooth and subtle flavour of the proper Italian ragù *from Bologna.*

The secret is long slow cooking – 2–3 hours in a heavy casserole – and, as usual, good-quality stewing or braising beef, trimmed of fat and chopped or minced, and real bacon or, better still, pancetta *(cured spiced belly of pork). To vary, add 2 oz (50 g) dried* porcini *(ceps) which you have soaked in hot (not boiling) water for about 15 minutes; these should go in, together with their soaking liquid, at the beginning of the slow simmering stage. A little grated nutmeg may also be added as a classic variation.*

Once the sauce is cooked, it can be cooled and stored in the refrigerator for 3 or 4 days, or frozen. Re-heat or thaw and cook gently for a further 15–20 minutes before serving with spaghetti, macaroni or tagliatelle – or use for baked lasagne.

Serves 4–6

1 lb (450 g) chuck steak or best-quality minced beef

3 tablespoons olive oil

4 oz (110 g) unsmoked gammon, green bacon or *pancetta*, de-rinded and chopped

1 medium onion, peeled and finely chopped

1 small carrot, peeled and finely chopped

1 stick celery, finely chopped

1 clove garlic, peeled and finely chopped (optional)

4 oz (110 g) chicken livers, trimmed and chopped

5 fl oz (150 ml) white or red wine

5 fl oz (150 ml) stock

1 × 14 oz (400 g) tin tomatoes

1 tablespoon tomato purée

3–4 tablespoons single cream

Pinch of salt

Freshly ground black pepper

About 1 lb (450 g) pasta, cooked, to serve

If using chuck steak, trim it of all visible fat and either put it through a mincer or chop it very finely in a food processor or by hand. Alternatively, ask the butcher to mince it for you.

In a large heavy saucepan or flameproof casserole heat the olive oil, add the gammon or bacon, onion, carrot and celery and sweat over a gentle heat until all the vegetables are soft. Turn up the heat a little and add the beef, garlic (if using) and chicken livers. Continue to cook, stirring all the time to spread the meat around until it has lost its pink rawness, but do not allow it to brown.

Now turn the heat up to moderate and pour in the wine and stock. Bring to the boil and reduce until the liquid has almost vanished. Add the tin of tomatoes with its juice (break up the tomatoes roughly with your stirring spoon), the tomato purée and cream. Turn the heat right down and let the sauce barely simmer, uncovered (no more than the occasional bubble should be visible), for 2–3 hours. Season with salt and pepper just before serving over the pasta.

Garlicky beefburgers with soured cream

These are not 100 per cent beef or real beefburgers but a very tasty adaptation which can be grilled, shallow-fried, baked in the oven or cooked outdoors over a barbecue. They could be served in baps, with salad leaves, or with potatoes, peas and puréed carrots.

Serves 4–6

1 lb (450 g) very lean minced beef

2–3 fat cloves garlic, peeled and crushed

1 small onion, peeled and very finely chopped or grated

1–2 tablespoons chopped mixed fresh herbs or 1–2 teaspoons mixed dried herbs

6 oz (175 g) slices bread, crusts removed

Pinch of salt

Freshly ground black pepper

1 egg, beaten

A little oil for frying

Soured cream

Pre-heat the oven to gas mark 5, 375°F (190°C).

Put the meat, garlic to taste, onion and herbs into a mixing bowl. Soak the bread thoroughly in a little water, then squeeze as dry as possible. Add the bread to the bowl and work everything together to combine, seasoning with salt and pepper and adding the egg as you go. At this stage you could put the mixture through a mincer or food processor for a smooth and even texture; however, the rougher texture is quite satisfactory. The mixture should be light and of a nice short consistency. Shape into burgers and gently fry them in a little oil until brown on both sides. Then transfer to a baking sheet, spoon a little soured cream on to each burger and cook in the oven for a further 15–20 minutes.

Oxtail stew

You need to start the day before to produce this rich tender meat dish with a beautifully flavoured glossy sauce which is almost totally free of fat. If the oxtail you buy is not prepared, ask you butcher to cut it into 2 inch (5 cm) pieces across the joints. Pig's trotters added to the stew will give it even more flavour. Serve with batons of carrot and turnip and plain boiled potatoes.

Serves 4–6

2½ lb (1.25 kg) oxtail, cut into 2 inch (5 cm) lengths

A little sunflower oil

2–3 carrots, scraped and cut into chunks

4 sticks celery, roughly chopped

8 oz (225 g) turnips, peeled and cut into chunks

1 bunch fresh herbs (bay leaf, parsley, thyme)

1 onion, peeled and quartered

About 10 fl oz (300 ml) home-made stock or water (do *not* use a stock cube)

About 10 fl oz (300 ml) red or white wine

Pinch of salt

Freshly ground black pepper

Chopped fresh parsley to garnish

Pre-heat the oven to gas mark 2, 300°F (150°C).

Wash the pieces of oxtail and pat them dry. Cut off as much of the visible fat as possible. In a large heavy frying-pan heat a little oil, add the oxtail and turn until brown all over. Using a slotted spoon transfer the meat to a heavy flameproof casserole. Now add a little more oil to the frying-pan and gently sweat out the carrots, celery and turnips. Add these to the meat in the casserole, together with the herbs and onion. Pour in enough stock or water and wine to cover. If you are using stock, do not add any extra seasoning; if you are using water, season lightly with salt and pepper, bearing in mind that the sauce will finally be reduced and concentrated. Heat the casserole on the top of the stove until the contents are scarcely simmering (do not allow to boil), cover with a tight-fitting lid and transfer to the oven. Leave to cook for 2 hours. Using a slotted spoon, remove the oxtail, draining well, put it into a dish, cool, cover and refrigerate. Strain the cooking liquid into a basin, cool, cover and refrigerate also. Discard the vegetables.

The following day pre-heat the oven again to gas mark 2, 300°F (150°C). While you are waiting for the oven to heat, skim all the fat from the surface of the cooking liquid: use a spoon to start with and complete the process by blotting the surface with kitchen paper. Then return the oxtail and cooking liquid to the casserole and continue cooking for 2 or 3 hours or until the oxtail is very tender but not actually falling apart. Do not allow the casserole to boil or the liquid will become cloudy. Meanwhile, prepare and cook the vegetables suggested as accompaniments in the introduction to this recipe.

To serve, use a slotted spoon to arrange the oxtail in the centre of a warmed serving platter. Keep warm. Boil the cooking liquid vigorously to reduce and concentrate the flavour. Check the seasoning and adjust if necessary. Pour the glossy dark sauce over the oxtail, surround with the vegetables, garnish with chopped parsley and serve immediately.

Kidney hotpot

Ox kidney has a good strong flavour and needs slow cooking. This is a substantial and nutritious hotpot, and makes an excellent inexpensive family meal.

Serves 6

12 oz (350 g) haricot beans

1–1½ lb (450–700 g) ox kidney

1 tablespoon vinegar

2 tablespoons olive oil

1 large onion, peeled and sliced

2 fat cloves garlic, peeled and chopped

Pinch of salt

Freshly ground black pepper

4 oz (110 g) mushrooms, wiped and sliced

1 pint (570 ml) home-made stock

White wine

2–3 teaspoons English mustard

Soak the beans overnight in plenty of cold water. Drain, cover with fresh cold water and simmer for 1½ hours (do not add any salt).

Skin and trim the kidney and cut into small pieces or thin slices. Soak in cold water to which you have added the vinegar for about 1 hour. Pre-heat the oven to gas mark 1, 275°F (140°C), for 1 hour before you need it.

When you are ready to cook, drain the kidney and pat it dry with kitchen paper. Heat 1 tablespoon of the olive oil in a heavy-bottomed frying-pan and gently fry the onion and garlic until soft but not brown. Place half the beans in a flameproof casserole, tip the onion and garlic over them and season well with salt and pepper. Add the remaining 1 tablespoon oil to the frying-pan and fry the kidney until lightly browned, adding the mushrooms for the final minute. Cover the onion and garlic layer in the casserole with the kidney and mushrooms, then cover these with the remaining beans. Pour the stock into the frying-pan and, as you heat it up to simmering point, scrape up the kidney juices which have stuck to the bottom. Pour this over the beans. Add a little wine until the liquid covers the contents of the casserole, and if the stock is not already well seasoned add a little more salt and pepper. Cover tightly and cook in the oven for at least 3 hours – even up to 6 hours the dish will not spoil. Take the casserole from the oven and stir in the mustard to taste before serving.

Variations
1 Add a little curry powder to the kidney at the frying stage.
2 Add a dash of chilli sauce in place of the mustard.
3 Use raw potatoes instead of beans. Peel the potatoes, cut them into chunks, and layer in the casserole as above. Cook for no more than 2½–3 hours. Obviously the bottom layer of potatoes becomes agreeably mushy as it absorbs the gravy and the top layer is slightly golden and baked – a lovely combination.

Calf's liver with onions Venetian-style

Not at all like the tough liver and watery onions that used to be served – to a chorus of groans – at our old school dinners, to be forced down with 'bullets' (rock-hard peas) and dried-up mashed potatoes, Dutch calf's liver is in a class of its own, and the slow-cooked onions in this recipe take on a delicious moist sweetness. The dish is good served with tender young peas and creamy mashed potatoes.

Serves 4

1¼ lb (550 g) calf's liver (preferably Dutch), very thinly sliced

4 tablespoons good-quality olive oil

2 oz (50 g) butter

2–3 large onions, peeled and very thinly sliced

Pinch of salt

Freshly ground black pepper

2–3 tablespoons chopped fresh parsley

Rinse the liver in cold running water and pat dry with kitchen paper.
  In a large heavy frying-pan heat 2 tablespoons of the oil and all of the butter, add the onions and cook very gently over a low heat, turning them from time to time, for about 45 minutes–1 hour or until they are totally soft and creamy.

Now heat the remaining oil in another frying-pan and fry the liver briskly for 5 minutes, turning once – cook for slightly less time if you prefer it rare. Season with a little salt and freshly ground black pepper. Meanwhile, stir nearly all the parsley into the onions. Divide the onions between 4 warmed plates, lay the slices of liver on top, pour over any meaty pan juices and garnish with the remaining parsley. Serve immediately.

Rhondda's meat loaf

This is a rather special version of a simple meat loaf which can be served cold for a summer's day main course or picnic. When sliced, it reveals a wonderful surprise layer of fluffy herbed omelette. Try experimenting with different herbs and seasonings according to your taste and their seasonal availability.

To serve, arrange slices of the loaf on a bed of salad leaves garnished with marigold petals. Accompany with a warm new potato salad and coleslaw.

Serves 4–6

4 eggs

1½ lb (700 g) lean skirt or chuck steak, minced

1 onion, peeled and very finely chopped

1 tablespoon finely chopped fresh oregano or 1 teaspoon dried oregano

1 tablespoon tomato purée

½ glass red wine

Dash of Worcestershire sauce

Pinch of salt

Freshly ground black pepper

A little oil for greasing

2 tablespoons chopped parsley

Pre-heat the oven to gas mark 4, 350°F (180°C).

Lightly beat 1 of the eggs and put it with the minced beef, onion, oregano, tomato purée, wine, Worcestershire sauce and salt and pepper to taste into a large bowl. With your hands mix and squeeze all these ingredients together very thoroughly.

Put about two thirds of the mixture into a lightly oiled 2 lb (900 g) loaf tin. Smooth it over and use the back of a spoon to hollow out a long, shallow, canoe shape.

Now make an omelette in the usual way with the 3 remaining eggs and, before you fold it into a roll, cover it with the parsley. Allow the omelette to cool, then place it in the hollow of the meat loaf and cover with the remaining mixture. Smooth it over and press down very gently.

Cover loosely with a double thickness of aluminium foil and bake in the oven for about 1–1¼ hours. Remove the foil and drain off any fat and liquid. When the loaf has cooled, invert it on to a plate and chill well before slicing.

Baked stuffed tripe and bacon roll

I used to love tripe and onions when I was a young girl, living in Lincolnshire. Sadly, in the South-west, where I have my home today, it seems impossible to buy really good honey-coloured tripe – and the usual way of cooking it results in a bland and rubbery stew or gratin. Here is a recipe idea I came across in a faded leaflet published by the British Medical Association! It's a very nourishing and unusual dish, and needs only vegetables – steamed cabbage, spring greens or spinach – to accompany it. (See page 47 for details of the three types of tripe.)

Serves 4

1½ lb (700 g) piece tripe

4 large potatoes

About 3 tablespoons chopped parsley

1 large onion, peeled and finely chopped

6 oz (175 g) wholewheat breadcrumbs

2 oz (50 g) lean smoked ham, finely chopped

Pinch of salt

Freshly ground black pepper

1 teaspoon freshly grated nutmeg

A little milk to moisten

4–6 rashers smoked bacon

4–5 tablespoons warmed tomato ketchup to serve

Ask your butcher how long you will need to cook the tripe (which is partly cooked when you buy it). Simmer it in a large pan of water for this time, or until tender. Drain well and set aside.

Boil and mash the potatoes in the usual way and add 1–2 tablespoons of the parsley, the onion, breadcrumbs and ham. Season with salt, pepper and nutmeg and mix thoroughly to combine the ingredients, adding a little milk to moisten.

Pre-heat the oven to gas mark 4, 350°F (180°C).

Lay the tripe, smooth side down, on a board and spread it with the potato mixture, leaving a ½ inch (1 cm) margin around the edge. Roll up the tripe tightly and tie with kitchen string. Place the roll on a trivet in a roasting tin, cover with overlapping rashers of bacon and bake in the oven for 1 hour.

To serve, slice the roll and arrange on a warmed platter. Pour over a little of the hot ketchup and scatter with the crumbled bacon from the top of the roll and the remaining chopped parsley.

Lamb

Boned leg of lamb stuffed with crabmeat

Crabmeat is a surprisingly wonderful stuffing for lamb. Ask your butcher to bone out a leg, and use the chopped bone to make stock. If possible, prepare the stock the day before to give the flavour time to reach its best. Serve the lamb with melting grilled ripe tomatoes, braised chicory and green lentils.

Serves 8–10

6 lb (2.75 kg) boned leg of lamb

A little sunflower oil

Stock:

Chopped bone and trimmings from the leg of lamb

2–3 carrots, peeled and finely chopped

2 sticks celery, sliced

2 medium onions, peeled and chopped

10 fl oz (300 ml) white wine

Pinch of salt

Freshly ground black pepper

1 bunch fresh herbs (bay leaf, parsley, thyme)

2–3 tomatoes, skinned and chopped (optional)

Stuffing:

½ oz (10 g) butter

1 small onion, peeled and very finely chopped

6 oz (175 g) fresh white crabmeat

6 oz (175 g) breadcrumbs

1 egg, beaten

Make the stock the day before, or at least several hours in advance. Pre-heat the oven to gas mark 7, 425°F (220°C). Put the chopped lamb bone and trimmings into a roasting tin and brown in the oven for 25 minutes. Turn off the oven and transfer the bones to a large saucepan. Put all the vegetables except the tomatoes into the roasting tin and cook them over a medium heat on top of the stove for 2–3 minutes or until brown. Add the vegetables to the bones in the saucepan. Pour off the fat in the roasting tin, splash in the wine and bring to the boil, stirring and scraping up all the coagulated browning juices. Pour this into the pan of bones and vegetables, add enough water to cover, season with salt and pepper and add the herbs and tomatoes (if using). Simmer for 1 hour, then strain. Return the stock to the saucepan and boil to reduce by about one third to concentrate the flavour. If making the stock on the day on which you are serving the roast lamb, pour it into a basin and cool quickly (see page 12). Using first a spoon, then absorbent kitchen paper, skim and blot the fat from the surface. If you are serving the lamb on the following day, chill the stock overnight before removing the fat.

To prepare the stuffing, melt the butter in a heavy-bottomed pan and gently fry the onion in it until soft but not brown. Add the onion to the remaining ingredients in a mixing bowl and combine thoroughly to produce a moist stuffing.

Wipe the lamb with dampened kitchen paper and pat dry.

Lay the opened leg, skin side down, on a board and spread the stuffing all over, working it well into any nooks and crannies. Roll up the meat, making sure that none of the stuffing spills out, secure with skewers and tie at 1–2 inch (2.5–5 cm) intervals with kitchen string. The meat should be at room temperature before you begin to cook.

Pre-heat the oven to gas mark 8, 450°F (230°C), brush the joint with oil and set on a rack or grid in a roasting tin. Place in the oven to seal and brown for 20 minutes. Turn the oven down to gas mark 4, 350°F (180°C), and continue to cook, allowing 25–30 minutes per lb (450 g) for a medium-rare boned joint and 30–35 minutes per lb (450 g) for a well-done one.

When the meat is cooked, take it from the oven and leave it, covered, in a warm place to rest for 15–20 minutes before carving. Meanwhile, re-heat the stock and boil to reduce somewhat. Combine it with the de-greased juices in the roasting tin to make the gravy (as described on page 54) and hand separately.

Roast leg of lamb with mint sauce

It makes my heart bleed to see top-quality meat in television advertisements showing the 'happy' housewife ruining the whole thing by making a quick 'gravy' from a stock cube, granules or cook-in sauce with its horrible manufactured and highly salty taste. No more time and very little expertise are needed to produce an intrinsically flavoursome gravy once you get into the habit of saving the water or juices from cooking your accompanying vegetables and combining them with the natural cooking juices of the meat.

Leg of lamb is one of the prime joints for roasting, and one of our best classic dishes is this simple roast served with a proper home-made fresh mint sauce. Recipes are given below for both Basic Mint Sauce and the more unusual Orange and Mint Sauce.

Serves 6–8

6 lb (2.75 kg) leg of lamb

A little sunflower oil

1 carrot, peeled and chopped

1 onion, peeled and chopped

1 tablespoon flour

Pre-heat the oven to gas mark 8, 450°F (230°C).

Wipe the joint with dampened kitchen paper and pat dry, then brush it with oil and set it on a rack or grid in a roasting tin. Cook in the oven for 20 minutes to brown and seal, then take the joint out of the oven. Turn down the heat to gas mark 4, 350°F (180°C).

Pop the chopped carrot and onion and the flour underneath the meat on the rack and return it to the oven. (The natural sugars in the vegetables will caramelise in the drippings from the meat, providing the basis for a good gravy.) Continue to roast the joint: for a medium-rare joint on the bone, roast for 1¼ hours (10–12 minutes per lb/450 g); for well-done meat, roast for approximately 1½ hours (13–15 minutes per lb/450 g). When it is cooked to your liking, remove from the oven and leave, covered, in a warm place to rest for 15–20 minutes before carving. Lamb produces less in the way of cooking juices than beef or pork, so you may need to supplement the cooking liquid from the potatoes and vegetables with some extra stock or wine for the gravy (see page 89).

Variations
Spiking lamb, as with Lamb in the Fog (page 90) is very popular. Make lots of incisions all over the joint and push into these one of the following:
1 Tinned anchovy fillets, first soaked in milk or water to lessen their saltiness, then patted dry and cut in half lengthways.
2 Slivers of peeled garlic and sprigs of rosemary.
Proceed to roast the joint in the usual way.

Basic Mint Sauce:

1 large bunch fresh mint

1–2 tablespoons sugar

A little vinegar

Chop the mint leaves quite finely, crush them in sugar to taste and pour over a little boiling water. Then add a good dash or two of vinegar and leave to cool.

Orange and Mint Sauce:

About 30 mint leaves

Juice of 1 orange and rind of ½ orange, very finely grated

1 teaspoon honey

1 teaspoon redcurrant jelly

3 tablespoons boiling water

2 tablespoons red wine vinegar

Very finely chop or pound the mint leaves. Add the grated orange rind, honey and redcurrant jelly. Pour over the boiling water, mix well and leave for 10 minutes. Now add the orange juice and vinegar. Chill before use.

Roast saddle of Welsh lamb

Very young Welsh lamb is one of spring's special delights. The saddle is a prime joint, and I think it is nicest classically roasted with a suggestion of fragrant herbs, although some people like it chined and stuffed. It is a sublime dish for a special dinner for four, and the simplest accompaniments are best. Spring is the time when you can serve tiny local or freshly lifted home-grown new potatoes and the first sweet fresh peas – and what could be nearer to heaven? A gratin of creamy potatoes would go well with the lamb too, and a serving of Welsh lavabread (see page 17) would be unusual but appropriate.

Do watch the lamb carefully while it is roasting – it is an expensive joint to spoil by overcooking (easily done, as I know to my cost). It should be crisp and golden-brown on the outside and tender rosy pink inside.

Serves 4

3–3½ lb (1.4–1.65 kg) saddle of Welsh lamb (prepared weight)

Pinch of salt

Freshly ground black pepper

A few sprigs fresh rosemary, thyme or lavender

A little butter, melted

1 carrot, peeled and chopped

1 onion, peeled and chopped

1 glass wine

About 10 fl oz (300 ml) home-made stock

If the saddle is not prepared, ask the butcher to remove the skin, leaving a thin layer of fat over the top of the saddle. He should then remove the excess fat from underneath the joint and trim the flank on each side, leaving enough to fold under the joint and cover the backbone. The fat should then be scored diagonally in both directions to form a diamond pattern; one tip of each diamond of fat can be flipped up slightly, so making an attractive design when golden and roasted. (Cut the fat only – not the meat.)

Before tying the saddle, wipe it with dampened kitchen paper and pat dry. Sprinkle the underside with a little salt and pepper and add a few sprigs of fresh herbs. Tie up the joint in the usual fashion, looping it at 2–3 inch (5–7.5 cm) intervals with kitchen string.

When you are ready to cook, pre-heat the oven to gas mark 8, 450°F (230°C). If the meat is chilled, allow it to come to room temperature before cooking. Set it on a rack or grid in a roasting tin and roast in the oven for

15–20 minutes. Quickly baste the joint with a little melted butter and throw the chopped carrot and onion into the roasting tin. (The natural sugars in the vegetables will caramelise in the dripping to add colour and flavour to the sauce.) Turn the oven down to gas mark 7, 425°F (220°C), and continue roasting, basting frequently, allowing approximately 10–12 minutes per lb (450 g) for a medium-rare and pink joint. You may have to turn the oven down to gas mark 6, 400°F (200°C) if the vegetables start to burn.

To test if the lamb is cooked, prod the saddle with your finger (don't pierce with a fork): the meat should feel resilient rather than soft, and the juices should now be running. Transfer the joint to a warmed plate and leave to rest for 15–20 minutes in a warm place.

Meanwhile, make the sauce. Skim off the fat in the roasting tin, then add the wine and bring to the boil, stirring and scraping up all the coagulated bits on the base of the tin and mashing the carrot and onion down into the liquid. Now add the stock and boil hard to reduce by at least half. Adjust the seasoning if necessary, strain and keep warm.

Cut the string from the joint and pour any juices that have run from it into the sauce. Take the joint to the table for carving and hand the sauce separately.

Variation
The saddle may also be finished with a delicious herbed crust.

1 small knob butter

1 tablespoon very finely chopped onion

2–3 tablespoons breadcrumbs

1 teaspoon chopped fresh rosemary, thyme or marjoram or 2 tablespoons chopped fresh parsley

A little finely grated lemon rind

While the joint is roasting, quickly melt the butter in a frying-pan and gently fry the onion until soft but not brown. Add the breadcrumbs and herbs and stir until the crumbs are golden. Add a little finely grated lemon rind. For the final 2–3 minutes of the joint's roasting time, spread the breadcrumb mixture over the top of the saddle to crisp.

Barbecued lamb in the fog

Determined, with characteristic British stiff upper lip, to ignore the thick swirling sea fog that engulfed my last barbecue, my male guests of the evening stood under a huge brolly and cooked this fabulous lamb.

Serves 8–10

1 large leg of lamb, boned and butterflied out, or 1 large shoulder of lamb, boned

6 cloves garlic, peeled and cut into long slivers

Thinly pared rind of 1 orange, cut into matchsticks

1 bunch fresh mint

Pinch of salt

Freshly ground black pepper

4 tablespoons lemon juice

4 tablespoons good-quality olive oil

Prepare the meat the day before. Wash it well, pat dry with kitchen paper, make a number of deep slits all over the meat and push into each slit a sliver of garlic, a matchstick of orange rind and a whole mint leaf. Season the meat with salt and pepper, then rub in the combined lemon juice and olive oil. Leave covered in a cool place for at least 1 day, turning occasionally and spooning over the marinade from the base of the dish.

When you are ready to cook, make sure the barbecue is spanking hot and good for at least an hour's cooking time. Oil the rack and set the meat on it as close as possible to the heat. Turn it and baste it with the remaining marinade from time to time as it cooks. The outside will look alarmingly black – but taste delicious – and the inside can be as pink and rare as you like, or you can continue to cook it right through.

Spiced grilled shoulder of lamb

This is a version of Cavalier's broil, a recipe dating back to the Royalist kitchens of the seventeenth century. I've adapted it from Elizabeth Ayrton's English Provincial Cooking, *in which she suggests that it is very good served with peas cooked with mint, creamed potatoes and redcurrant jelly.*

I particularly like the idea of the final grilling which reduces the fattiness of this cut of lamb, but if your grill is not large enough to accommodate the joint you will have to turn your oven up to maximum for the final stages of cooking.

Serves 4–6

3½–4 lb (1.6–1.8 kg) shoulder of lamb

3 tablespoons sunflower oil

12 oz (350 g) mushrooms, stems removed, wiped and finely sliced

Juice of ½ lemon

Juice of ½ orange

Pinch of salt

Freshly ground black pepper

Spice Mixture:

1 fresh red chilli, de-seeded and very finely chopped

1 inch (2.5 cm) cube fresh root ginger, peeled and grated or very finely chopped

1 clove garlic, peeled and very finely chopped

1 teaspoon ground coriander seeds

Salt

Freshly ground black pepper

2 tablespoons sunflower oil

Pre-heat the oven to gas mark 6, 400°F (200°C).

Wipe the lamb with dampened kitchen paper and pat dry. Set it on a rack in a roasting tin. Rub all over with 1 tablespoon of the oil and roast in the oven for 40–50 minutes.

Meanwhile, heat the remaining 2 tablespoons oil in a heavy frying-pan and gently fry the mushrooms in it without browning them. When they are cooked through but still firm, add the lemon and orange juices and season lightly with salt and pepper. Bring up to just under simmering point, then set aside and keep warm.

Put the spice mixture ingredients in the bowl of a food processor or liquidiser and whizz until smooth. Set aside. Now light the grill. Take the lamb out of the oven and, using a very sharp knife, score 3 cuts at equal intervals down to the bone on each side of the joint. Pack the spice mixture well into each scored cut and put the joint on the rack over the grill pan. (Save the juices in the roasting tin.) Grill the lamb, turning it from time to time, for about 20 minutes, when the meat near the bone should be rosy pink and the skin crisp and brown.

Meanwhile, blot or skim the fat off the meat juices in the roasting tin and re-heat these juices.

Put the joint on a warmed serving dish, pour over the re-heated roasting juices, then pour over the hot mushrooms. Serve immediately.

Lamb with olives

This is a superb Italian recipe which is extremely quick to cook. The sauce is piquant but it should be said that, to enjoy this dish, you must love olives as they are definitely not an optional ingredient. You could serve Lamb with Olives with fresh crusty bread, or fried potatoes, and a green salad.

Serves 4

1½ lb (700 g) tender lean boneless leg or loin steaks or fillets of lamb

2–3 oz (50–75 g) flour

6 tablespoons good-quality olive oil

Pinch of salt

6 oz (175 g) black olives, stoned and chopped

Pinch of dried oregano or 1 teaspoon chopped fresh oregano

½ fresh red chilli or 1 small green pepper, de-seeded and finely chopped

Juice of 1 lemon

Wipe the lamb with dampened kitchen paper and pat dry.

Turn the meat in the flour to coat lightly. Heat the olive oil in a large heavy frying-pan and fry the lamb in it briskly for 3–5 minutes, turning once. Turn down the heat, pour off most of the oil, then salt the lamb and add the olives, oregano, chilli or green pepper and half the lemon juice. Continue cooking, stirring the olives around from time to time, for a further 3–4 minutes, depending on whether you prefer your lamb pink inside or cooked right through. Taste and add more lemon juice if you wish. Serve immediately.

Minty lamb in filo pastry

The scent rushes at you when you plunge into these crispy pastry packages. Using filo pastry makes this lamb en croûte far less rich and filling than if you were to use puff pastry. The recipe method is very versatile too – try other combinations of herbs and seasonings, for instance fresh rosemary and garlic, slices of feta cheese, or finely chopped mushrooms and shallots cooked in a little sherry. If you are using frozen filo pastry, the packet can be re-frozen after you have peeled off the sheets you need for this recipe. Serve the pastry packages with salad leaves and new potatoes dressed with herbed soured cream.

Serves 4

4 boned leg steaks or fillets of lamb, trimmed of all visible fat

About 4–5 tablespoons sunflower oil

2 tablespoons chopped fresh mint

2 fat cloves garlic, peeled and very finely chopped

8 sheets filo pastry, thawed if frozen and cut in half to form 16 squares

Pinch of salt

Freshly ground black pepper

4 medium mushrooms, wiped and thinly sliced

4 ripe tomatoes, halved

Wipe the lamb steaks or fillets with dampened kitchen paper and pat dry. Heat a little sunflower oil in a frying-pan, add the meat and brown it for 1–2 minutes on each side. Drain on kitchen paper and allow to cool a little. Cut a slit horizontally in the side of each steak and push in some mint and garlic.

Pre-heat the oven to gas mark 6, 400°F (200°C).

Meanwhile prepare the filo pastry. Using a pastry brush, brush one side of a sheet of the pastry all over with sunflower oil. Put another sheet on top and brush with more oil. Continue in the same way with 2 more sheets so that you have 4 oiled sheets in all for the first package. Place a lamb steak in the centre, season lightly with salt and pepper and arrange a layer of overlapping mushroom slices along the top of it. Fold over the 2 diagonally facing corners of the pastry package, brush with a little oil, then fold over the remaining 2 corners, finishing with a little more oil. Form the 3 other packages and place them all on a baking sheet. Bake for 25–30 minutes or until crisp and golden. Sprinkle the cut surface of the tomatoes with a little oil and black pepper and, after the parcels have been cooking for 15 minutes, add these to the baking sheet. Serve straight from the oven.

Spiced skewered lamb

You can find wooden skewers – they look like giant cocktail sticks – in good kitchen shops.

Serves 4

1 small onion, peeled and roughly chopped

1 lb (450 g) lean lamb, cut into small cubes

1 tablespoon ground or crushed coriander seeds

4–6 cloves, ground or crushed

1 inch (2.5 cm) piece fresh root ginger, peeled and very finely chopped

2 fat cloves garlic, peeled and very finely chopped

Pinch of salt

Plenty of freshly ground black pepper

Oil for greasing

Put the onion into a food processor and whizz for 10 seconds. Add the cubes of lamb and process for a further 20 seconds. Add the remaining ingredients and whizz until you have a well amalgamated burger-type mixture.

Alternatively, if you do not have a food processor, ask your butcher to mince the lamb. Finely chop or grate the onion and, using your hands, squeeze and knead it and the remaining ingredients into the meat.

Now take a small handful of the mixture and shape and mould it around and along a wooden skewer so that you form a fairly fat sausage shape 4–5 inches (10–12.5 cm) long. Continue filling skewers in this way until the mixture is used up – there should be enough for 8–10 skewers. Cover the skewers and leave them in a cool place for at least 2 hours, or overnight, for the flavours to develop and mingle.

Pre-heat the grill or barbecue and oil the rack thoroughly. Put the skewers on the rack and cook for about 10 minutes, turning them from time to time – they can be slightly pink inside if you wish. Serve sizzling hot with Cool Yoghurt and Mint Sauce (see page 216) or allow them to cool and serve them as part of a picnic meal.

Lamb under-roast with apricots and cider

'Under-roast' is a Cornish expression which describes a traditional, delicious, one-pot method of stretching a relatively small amount of good-quality lean beef with a generous flavouring of turnip or swede, onion and potato. In fact it is no more a real 'roast' than a pot roast – and in intention is comparable with a good northern meat and potato pie. This is an adaptation, using lamb, apricots and cider instead of beef and water or stock. It produces a sweet and meaty gravy and is well-tempered enough to ignore in a low oven without spoiling until you are ready to eat.

Serves 4–6

1½–2 lb (700–900 g) lean leg or loin steaks of lamb

About 2 tablespoons seasoned flour for coating

1 tablespoon finely chopped mixed fresh herbs (such as parsley with marjoram, thyme, sage, as available) or 1–2 teaspoons mixed dried herbs

2 medium onions, peeled and sliced

1½ lb (700 g) young turnips, peeled and sliced

4 oz (110 g) dried apricots, chopped

Pinch of salt

Freshly ground black pepper

2–2½ lb (900 g–1.25 kg) potatoes, peeled and sliced into thin rounds

About 1 pint (570 ml) dry cider

1 tablespoon double cream (optional)

Squeeze of lemon juice

Pre-heat the oven to gas mark 5, 375°F (190°C).

Trim any visible fat from the lamb and cut into even-sized pieces about 2 × 4 inches (5 × 10 cm). Dust them lightly with seasoned flour and pack them in one layer in a deep roasting tin. Cover with the herbs, then the onions, turnips and apricots. Season lightly with salt and pepper and finish with an overlapping layer or two of potatoes. Pour in the cider until it reaches the beginning of the potato layer, cover loosely with aluminium foil and bake in the oven for about 1½ hours or until everything is tender when you test it with a skewer. Keep warm in a low oven until you are ready to eat.

Now carefully pour off all the cooking liquid into a saucepan and boil hard to reduce by half, to thicken and concentrate the sauce: there should be about 10 fl oz (300 ml) remaining. Take off the heat and whisk in 1 tablespoon cream (if using), check the seasoning and add a squeeze of lemon juice. Arrange the lamb and vegetables on warmed plates, pour over a little sauce and serve immediately, handing the remaining sauce in a jug.

Lamb's kidneys in baked potatoes

Slowly baked in the hollowed middle of jacket potatoes, the kidneys release their rich distinctive juices into the potato flesh. If you wish, this dish can be partly prepared in advance in the kitchen and each kidney-filled potato wrapped in aluminium foil and pushed into the embers of a barbecue fire for an hour to finish cooking. Carrots, slowly braised in the oven with a little brown sugar, and a green salad are good accompaniments.

Serves 4

4 large baking potatoes, scrubbed and lightly oiled

4 lamb's kidneys, skinned and core removed

Freshly ground black pepper

Dijon mustard

4 rashers streaky bacon

Pre-heat the oven to gas mark 5, 375°F (190°C).

Bake the potatoes in the oven for 1 hour. Cool slightly to handle, then slice off a 'lid' from the top of each potato and, using a spoon or scoop, make a hollow in each one.

Rinse the kidneys in cold runnning water and pat dry with kitchen paper. Season each one with pepper and mustard, and wrap it in a rasher of bacon. Put a wrapped kidney into each potato, replace the lid, wrap loosely in aluminium foil and continue baking in the oven for a further hour.

To serve, peel back the foil and set the lids askance.

Noisettes of lamb with aubergines

Learning to prepare your own noisettes will prove a useful and rewarding skill which will save money and provide bones for stock. However, noisettes are available ready-prepared at some supermarkets, or you could ask your butcher to make them up for you. Aubergines and lamb are a fine partnership, as you will know if you like moussaka. This dish goes well with new potatoes.

Serves 4

4 × 4 oz (110 g) thick noisettes of lamb or 1½ lb (700 g) best end of neck of lamb, chined only

1 tablespoon finely chopped fresh herbs (especially oregano), plus a few sprigs to garnish

2–3 oz (50–75 g) feta cheese, crumbled

2 aubergines, sliced

Salt

3–4 tablespoons good-quality olive oil

2 cloves garlic, peeled and finely chopped

Freshly ground black pepper

2–3 onions, peeled and thinly sliced into rings

1 quantity Fresh Tomato Sauce (see page 214) to serve

If you are preparing your own noisettes, scatter the herbs and cheese over the meat before rolling it up tightly. Tie and refrigerate to firm up for 1 hour before slicing the roll of meat between each piece of string.

If using prepared noisettes, remove the string, cut away the fat, make a slit in the side of each noisette, push in some herbs and feta cheese, and tie up again.

Sprinkle the slices of aubergine with salt and leave for 30 minutes to allow the juices to exude. Rinse, drain and pat dry with kitchen paper.

When you are ready to cook, heat some of the olive oil in a heavy frying-pan. Have ready a large warmed serving plate. Fry the aubergines on both sides, then add the garlic, sprinkle with a little salt and pepper and shake the pan as you cook everything through for a few minutes. Carefully transfer to the warmed serving plate and keep warm. Add a little more oil to the pan and gently fry the onions. Drain well and keep warm.

Meanwhile, heat the grill. Brush the noisettes with a little oil and grill under a medium heat for 8–10 minutes on each side or until they are golden-brown and cooked through. Remove the string. Re-heat the Fresh Tomato Sauce.

Pour a little sauce on to each of 4 warmed dinner plates and make an attractive arrangement of overlapping aubergine slices, then set the noisettes on the plates in nests of the onions and garnish with a few sprigs of fresh herbs. Serve immediately.

Lamb kebabs with lime juice and yoghurt

Delightfully simple to prepare and quick to cook indoors or outdoors on a barbecue, these tangy kebabs could be served with steamed garlic-infused couscous and speckled with lots of chopped fresh mint. You can use a lemon if limes are unavailable. A lively salad of watercress and tomato is a good accompaniment.

Serves 4

1–1½ lb (450–700 g) boned leg of lamb

A little sunflower oil

2–3 medium courgettes

Marinade:

5 fl oz (150 ml) Greek yoghurt

4–6 spring onions, trimmed and very finely sliced, including all the good green parts

Pinch of cayenne pepper

2 inch (5 cm) piece fresh root ginger, peeled and grated

2 fat cloves garlic, peeled and crushed

Juice of 1 lime and a little grated rind

Pinch of salt

Freshly ground black pepper

First trim the lamb of all visible fat and cut it into 1 inch (2.5 cm) cubes. In a glass or earthenware bowl whisk together the marinade ingredients and add the cubes of lamb, making sure that each piece is smothered in the mixture. Cover the bowl and leave in a cool place for 3–4 hours or overnight.

When you are ready to cook, light the grill or prepare the barbecue and oil 4 long kebab skewers. Wipe the courgettes and cut them into 1 inch (2.5 cm) thick slices. Thread these slices alternately with cubes of marinated lamb on to the skewers and place on the grill or barbecue rack to cook for about 10 minutes, turning them and basting with a little sunflower oil from time to time. Serve immediately.

Braised liver with heaven and earth

Heaven (apples) and Earth (potatoes) is a German dish which goes beautifully with tender stuffed braised liver and its gravy. My busy mother would cheat and use a packet stuffing to save time, adding a few fresh herbs, a little grated onion and a smidgin of lemon rind – with excellent results. If you get your timing right, a little of the potato and apple cooking liquid could be added to the braised liver stock and boiled hard in a separate saucepan until reduced somewhat, so producing a truly excellent and flavoursome gravy. This is a homely winter's night main course for which you can, if you wish, use inexpensive liver (see page 46 for information on types of liver).

Serves 4

1 lb (450 g) lamb's liver, trimmed and sliced

4–5 rashers streaky bacon

6 oz (175 g) breadcrumbs

1 medium onion, peeled and very finely chopped or grated

½ tablespoon finely chopped parsley

½ tablespoon finely chopped mixed fresh herbs or 1 teaspoon mixed dried herbs

Pinch of salt

Freshly ground black pepper

A little grated lemon rind

1 small egg, beaten

Milk

Oil for greasing

A little stock

Heaven and Earth:

5 medium potatoes

1–2 apples, peeled, cored and sliced

2 oz (50 g) butter

Pinch of salt

Freshly ground black pepper

Pre-heat the oven to gas mark 4, 350°F (180°C).

Wash the liver in cold running water and pat dry with kitchen paper. De-rind the bacon. Mix together the breadcrumbs, onion, parsley, herbs, salt, pepper and grated lemon rind and bind with the egg, adding a little milk if necessary.

Cover each slice of liver with some of the stuffing and lay the slices on the base of a lightly oiled baking dish. Cover with the bacon rashers, pour a little stock around and bake in the oven for at least 45 minutes. The cooking time will be affected by the type and thickness of both the liver and of the baking dish you are using: you could help things along by using a flameproof casserole dish and first bringing the liver up to barely simmering on top of the stove before transferring it to the oven.

Meanwhile, make the Heaven and Earth. Peel the potatoes and boil in the usual way. After 10 minutes or so, add the apples. When both potatoes and apples are cooked, drain, add the butter, salt and pepper and mash them thoroughly. Serve piping hot with the braised liver.

Lancashire hotpot

If you are feeling particularly extravagant, you can add half a dozen oysters to this traditional stew – an authentic addition in past times when they were also added to steak and kidney pies.

Serves 4–6

8 best end of neck lamb chops

2 oz (50 g) home-made dripping or butter

1 small bunch herbs (bay leaf, parsley, sage)

4 large onions, peeled and chopped

2 lb (900 g) carrots, scrubbed or peeled and chopped

Pinch of salt

Freshly ground black pepper

2 oz (50 g) flour

About 1 pint (570 ml) stock or water

1–2 teaspoons sugar

6 oysters (optional)

2 lb (900 g) potatoes, peeled and sliced into ¼ inch (5 mm) thick rounds

1 oz (25 g) butter, melted

Pre-heat the oven to gas mark 4, 350°F (180°C).

Wipe and trim the chops. Use a little of the dripping or butter to grease a deep casserole and put the bunch of herbs in the bottom. Heat the remaining dripping or butter in a large frying-pan and brown the chops in it on both sides. Remove with a spatula and stand them in the casserole on top of the herbs, thick ends downwards and bones pointing towards the top. The ends of the bones should come 1–2 inches (2.5–5 cm) below the top of the casserole; however, if you are using a shallow casserole dish, lay the chops on the bottom.

Soften the onions in the frying-pan, then remove with a slotted spoon, draining well. Repeat the process with the carrots. Pack these vegetables around the chops, seasoning well with salt and pepper. Add the flour to the fat remaining in the frying-pan and cook it over a gentle heat for a few minutes. Gradually add the stock or water, stirring continually to make a smooth thick gravy, then add sugar, salt and pepper to taste. Pour into the casserole; it should just cover the bones. If you are using oysters, add these now with their juices. Then arrange the slices of potato in an overlapping pattern over the top, season with salt and pepper, brush with melted butter, cover and bake in the oven for 2 hours. To finish, raise the heat to gas mark 6, 400°F (200°C), remove the cover and continue to bake for 15–20 minutes or until the potatoes are crisp and golden-brown. Serve hot.

Grilled lamb's kidneys with mashed potato and celeriac

A beautiful way to eat these delectable kidneys. If you cannot find celeriac, try mashing the potatoes with an equal quantity of boiled swede or parsnip. Grilled tomatoes and mushrooms with crisp bacon or a good Lincolnshire sausage are fine accompaniments.

Serves 4

1 lb (450 g) potatoes, scrubbed

Salt

1 lb (450 g) celeriac, peeled

Dash of lemon juice

5 fl oz (150 ml) hot milk

Freshly ground black pepper

A little olive oil

8 lamb's kidneys

A little Dijon mustard

First prepare the potatoes and celeriac. Cook the potatoes in their skins in boiling salted water until just tender, drain, cool, peel and mash. Meanwhile, cut the celeriac into chunks and, to prevent them from discolouring, drop them into a bowl of water acidulated with a dash of lemon juice as you go. Cook them also in boiling salted water until tender, drain and mash. Mix the 2 mashed vegetables together, put them in a large saucepan over a gentle heat to dry out a little, then beat in the hot milk and season well with salt and pepper. Keep warm.

Now pre-heat the grill and oil the grill rack.

Skin each kidney and cut lengthways almost all the way through to open out butterfly-fashion. Use small scissors to snip out the white core, rinse in cold running water and pat dry with kitchen paper. Brush the kidneys with a little oil, place cut side upwards on the grill rack and spread just a little mustard on each one. Grill fairly gently for about 3 minutes, then turn them over and grill for a further 2–3 minutes, depending on your taste. (I like them to be pink in the middle.)

Serve 2 kidneys per person on warmed plates with a portion of mashed potato and celeriac and the grill pan juices poured over.

Pork
and
Ham

Pork cooked in milk

White meats cooked in milk used to be regarded as good for the elderly convalescent or for children, but please don't let this put you off such dishes. The fact is that the acid in milk has an astonishing tenderising effect on pork, as well as producing an almost fat-free flavoursome joint of juicy succulence. This is partly because the joint is not sealed by browning first. It is a slow-simmering dish; the milk in which the meat is cooked produces the sauce. Serve with leeks and broad beans.

Serves 6

3 lb (1.4 kg) boned rolled leg or loin of pork

2 fat cloves garlic, peeled and cut lengthways into slivers

1–2 teaspoons coriander seeds, crushed or ground

A little salt

1 oz (25 g) butter

1 stick celery, finely sliced

2 shallots, peeled and chopped

1 small piece turnip or carrot

1 bunch herbs (bay leaf, marjoram, parsley)

1½–2 pints (900 ml–1.1 litres) whole milk

Freshly ground white pepper

Parsley sprigs to garnish

Pre-heat the oven to gas mark 2, 300°F (150°C).

Trim the fat off the joint, wipe it with dampened kitchen paper and pat dry. Make deep incisions all over the surface. Dip the slivers of garlic into the coriander and push these into the incisions in the pork. Rub the joint all over with the remaining coriander, working it into any cracks or gaps you can find, then rub a little salt all over too.

Over a gentle heat melt the butter in a flameproof casserole large enough to hold the joint and sweat out the celery, shallots and turnip or carrot. When they are soft but not brown, put the meat on top and add the bunch of herbs. In a separate saucepan heat the milk until just under simmering point, add a good grinding of pepper and pour it over the meat. Cover the casserole with a double thickness of aluminium foil or a tight-fitting lid and cook in the oven for about 3 hours, turning the meat from time to time.

Remove the meat from the milk and turn the oven up to gas mark 6, 400°F

(200°C). Transfer the meat to a roasting tin and return it to the oven to brown for a further 30 minutes.

Meanwhile, make the sauce. Do not discard the 'curtains' – that is to say, the golden skin on top of the milk in the casserole: this contains a high proportion of valuable nutrients. Strain the milk through a fine sieve, making sure that you push all the milky solids through. Cool the milk quickly and skim off the fat. Bring the milk to the boil in a saucepan and continue to cook until it has reduced and thickened: this makes a deliciously flavoured sauce.

To serve, slice the pork and arrange it on warmed plates with a little of the sauce. Garnish with parsley.

Roast rolled leg of pork with stuffed baked apples and sweet and sour plum sauce

This is a super-light and fresh way to cook a joint of pork – with the usual bonus of cold slices to serve the next day accompanied by spicy chutneys, pickles, salads and fresh crusty bread or potato cakes from the griddle.

Serves 6–8

4 lb (1.8 kg) boneless rolled leg joint of pork

Freshly ground black pepper

6 medium apples (preferably Granny Smith), wiped and cored

Stir-fried rice with mange-tout, bean sprouts and spring onions to serve

Sweet and Sour Plum Sauce:

1 lb (450 g) plums

5 fl oz (150 ml) white wine

2 cloves

2–3 teaspoons honey

1 teaspoon ground ginger

Squeeze of lemon juice

Stuffing:

1 small onion, very finely chopped

A little sunflower oil

8 oz (225 g) wholewheat breadcrumbs

½ teaspoon ground cinnamon

¼ teaspoon ground allspice

1 tablespoon grated lemon or orange rind

2 oz (50 g) pine nuts

2 oz (50 g) walnuts, finely chopped

Freshly ground black pepper

First prepare the Plum Sauce. Wash the plums and poach them in a saucepan with the white wine and cloves until they are soft and the skins are splitting. Put a fine-meshed sieve over a small basin and pour the plums and their cooking liquid through: use a wooden spoon to press through all the pulp, then discard the stones and skins. Return the purée to the saucepan, add the honey and ginger and boil to reduce by one third. You should now have a thick sauce of pouring consistency. Add a squeeze or two of lemon juice to taste and, if necessary, a little more honey and ginger until the sauce has an agreeable sweet and sour taste. Set aside. The sauce can, of course, be prepared some time in advance.

When you are ready to cook, pre-heat the oven to gas mark 3, 325°F (170°C). Wipe the joint with dampened kitchen paper and pat dry. Put the joint on a rack over a roasting tin, season with plenty of black pepper and roast in the oven for 2 hours or until the meat is thoroughly cooked. (This is the slow roasting method to avoid shrinkage.) Check whether the joint is ready by piercing with a fine skewer: any juices that run out should be clear.

Meanwhile, prepare the stuffing. Cook the onion in a little oil until soft and transparent, then mix with all the remaining stuffing ingredients. Make sure that you have a generous cored cavity in each apple and push some stuffing into each one. Stand them in a baking dish, pour 1–2 tablespoons water around them and bake in the oven with the pork for the last 30–40 minutes of its cooking time.

When the meat is cooked, allow it to stand for 10 minutes before carving into thin slices. Re-heat the Plum Sauce. Very carefully slice the slightly cooled apples horizontally into ½ inch (1 cm) thick rounds. Pour pools of Plum Sauce on to each warmed plate and arrange overlapping slices of pork and stuffed apple alternately in a generous and decorative fan shape. Serve immediately with a huge dish of stir-fried rice with mange-tout, bean sprouts and spring onions.

Roast pork with crackling and apple sauce

Although I am very much in favour of reducing the amount of fat in our diet, it does seem a shame to miss out on the occasional full-blown roast joint of pork with proper crackling. These traditional roasts seem to stretch and stretch to feed Sunday lunchtime all-comers and family gatherings, and are a satisfying break from the snatch-and-grab food in our busy lives.

So here is the method for a succulent leg or loin of pork with crisp crackling and the minimum of fat. A tart apple sauce offsets the richness of the meat, but for an interesting change you might like to try slices or a purée of papaya (see page 135) which is also an excellent accompaniment.

Serve the roast with steamed Brussels sprouts, braised red cabbage and potatoes – and remember to save the cooking water from the sprouts and potatoes for making the gravy.

Serves 6–8 or more

1 leg or loin of pork

Salt

2 carrots, peeled and sliced

1 onion, peeled and sliced

1 oz (25 g) white flour

Stock for the gravy (optional)

Apple Sauce:

1 lb (450 g) Bramley or other cooking apples

1 thin strip orange or lemon rind

1 oz (25 g) caster sugar

½ oz (10 g) butter

Pre-heat the oven to gas mark 5, 375°F (190°C).

Wipe the joint with dampened kitchen paper and pat dry. Using the point of a very sharp kitchen, craft or Stanley knife, score the pork skin, making long strokes about ½ inch (1 cm) apart; take care not to penetrate the lean meat. Alternatively ask your butcher to score it for you. The joint must be at room temperature and dry before you start to cook. Do not rub the skin with oil or fat or your crackling will be a failure; instead rub it all over with a little salt for crispness.

Put the carrots, onion and flour in a roasting tin and set the joint, rind side up, on a rack or grid above them. (The natural sugars in the vegetables will caramelise in the dripping to add colour and flavour, and the flour will absorb the dripping for a nice brown gravy thickening.) Roast in the oven for 35 minutes per lb (450 g) plus 35 minutes: it is essential to cook pork thoroughly. If you are using a meat thermometer, a temperature 185–194°F (85–90°C) indicates that the pork is well done.

While the pork is cooking, make the Apple Sauce. Wipe the apples but do not peel them. Quarter and core them, and cut into slices. Cook gently in a saucepan with 2–3 tablespoons water and the lemon rind for about 10 minutes or until they are soft. Strain them through a fine sieve, pushing hard on the peel to extract every drop of flavour. Return this purée to the pan over a gentle heat, add the sugar and stir until dissolved, then continue cooking very gently to dry the purée somewhat. Stir in the butter and keep warm until you are ready to serve.

When the joint is done, remove it from the oven and leave to rest in a warm place for 15 minutes before carving. If the crackling is not crisp, remove it now in one piece and either grill it or turn up the oven and bake it for a further 15 minutes.

Meanwhile, pour all the surplus fat from the roasting tin, leaving behind the dark coagulated cooking juices. Stir in a little vegetable cooking water or stock to make a nice thin gravy. Simmer for a few minutes on top of the stove and strain into a gravy boat or jug. Carve the pork and serve straight away with the strips of crackling and Apple Sauce.

Chilli pork and spinach stir-fry

Of the many stir-fries I love to compose, this powerful tasting spicy dish has the most vibrant colour. It makes a stunning appearance served on large white dinner plates, and is a lightish main course if accompanied by a side dish of plain rice. Remember with stir-frying to prepare all your ingredients before you begin to cook, and use one or two spatulas to keep everything moving briskly around the hot pan. Because only relatively small quantities of ingredients can be stir-fried at one time, this sort of dish is usually suitable only for two people as a main course.

Serves 2

6–8 oz (175–225 g) pork tenderloin or fillet

½–1 fresh red chilli, de-seeded and finely chopped

2 tablespoons dark soy sauce

1 fat clove garlic, peeled and very finely chopped

Freshly ground white pepper

2–3 tablespoons sunflower or peanut (groundnut) oil

1 small red pepper, halved lengthways, de-seeded and cut into 2 × ¼ inch (5 × 0.5 cm) strips

1 bunch spring onions, trimmed and sliced on the diagonal, including all the good green parts

4 oz (110 g) mange-tout, topped, tailed and cut in half

6 handfuls spinach leaves, ribs removed and roughly chopped

4 oz (110 g) sprouted mung beans

3 tomatoes, skinned and sliced

Trim the meat of all visible fat, wipe with dampened kitchen paper and pat dry. If using tenderloin, slice into very thin rounds, then cut them in half to make crescents. If using fillet, slice it into thin strips.

In a small bowl mix together the chilli, soy sauce, garlic and pepper. Assemble the remaining ingredients.

Put 2 large dinner plates to warm, and have ready another warm plate lined with a sheet of kitchen paper.

Heat a large wok or heavy frying-pan. When it is hot, pour in the oil, swirl it around, then add the pork and stir-fry briskly for 1 minute or until the pork has turned white. Using a slotted spoon transfer the pork to the plate lined with kitchen paper to drain. Now throw in the red pepper, spring onions,

Raised game pie (page 170), Special domed individual steak and mushroom pie (page 67), and Ham, parsley and sweetcorn pie (page 117)

(centre spread) Game pudding (page 160), Roast goose (page 144), and Braised partridge with pumpkin (page 152)

mange-tout, spinach and mung beans and stir-fry for a further minute. Add the soy sauce mixture followed by the tomatoes and stir-fry for 30 seconds. Now return the pork to the wok and continue to stir-fry everything for a final 20–30 seconds.

Tip the contents of the wok on to the 2 warmed dinner plates and serve immediately.

Grilled pork with sweet and sour plum sauce

Sharp fruity sauces always go well with pork and this one, which is particularly colourful, can be prepared in advance and re-heated. Serve with plain boiled rice – individual moulds look most attractive with this dish.

Serves 4

4 pork topside leg or shoulder steaks

1 tablespoon dark soy sauce

1 tablespoon clear honey

1 tablespoon Dijon mustard

1–2 bunches large spring onions, trimmed, green parts removed and white parts cut in half lengthways

A little sunflower oil

Sweet and Sour Plum Sauce to serve (see page 107)

Trim the pork steaks, wipe with dampened kitchen paper and pat dry. Put them into a wide shallow dish with the combined soy sauce, honey and mustard. Cover and leave in a cool place for 2–3 hours.

Meanwhile, prepare the Sweet and Sour Plum Sauce.

When you are ready to cook the meat, pre-heat the grill to a medium heat and oil the grill rack. Grill the pork steaks for about 10 minutes on each side, depending on their thickness. Half-way through the cooking time, place the spring onions on a square of aluminium foil, sprinkle them with a little sunflower oil and grill them alongside the steaks until they are slightly soft and golden.

To serve, pour a pool of Sweet and Sour Plum Sauce on to each of 4 warmed plates and lay the steaks on the sauce with the spring onions.

Kidney hotpot (page 78), and Peppery grilled chicken with lemon (page 131)

Home-made herbed sausages

Not all sausages need skins! And although some commercially made sausages are excellent, most are rather poor. Making your own is easy and rewarding – and you have the assurance of knowing exactly what your sausages contain. You can fill skins with this mixture if you wish (see page 17).

As a variation try flavouring the sausages with chopped fresh coriander and garlic instead of sage and nutmeg. You can also bake them in the oven rather than frying them if you prefer.

Serve with a gratin of leeks and potatoes.

Serves 4

1 small onion, peeled

1 lb (450 g) lean pork, cubed

8 oz (225 g) belly pork, de-rinded and roughly chopped

2 oz (50 g) cashew nuts, roughly ground or chopped

1 tablespoon finely chopped fresh sage

Pinch of grated nutmeg

Pinch of salt

Freshly ground black pepper

A little oil for frying

Put the onion into a food processor and whizz for 10 seconds. Add all the cubed and chopped pork and process for a further 30 seconds. Now add all the remaining ingredients except the oil and whizz until you have a smoothish sausagemeat mixture.

Alternatively, chop or grate the onion very finely and pass it and the meat through a mincer two or three times, adding the remaining sausagemeat ingredients for the final time.

Heat a little oil in a large non-stick frying-pan and fry a nut of the mixture in it until golden-brown all over; taste this to check the flavour and add more seasoning and/or herbs to the remaining mixture if appropriate. Shape the mixture into generous sausage shapes and fry them gently, turning occasionally, until golden-brown and cooked right through. Drain on kitchen paper before serving.

Toad in the hole

For this all-time favourite, find a butcher or food shop which makes or sells really good-quality unadulterated sausages – or see the recipes for home-made pork sausages on page 113 of this book. Braised cabbage and roast onions are excellent accompaniments.

Serves 4

1 quantity Yorkshire Pudding Batter (see page 55)

1 handful finely chopped fresh herbs or a little finely chopped onion (optional)

A little oil or poultry dripping

1 lb (450 g) pork, beef or game sausages

4 lamb's kidneys, skinned and core removed (optional)

Prepare the Yorkshire Pudding Batter at least 1 hour in advance, adding a handful of chopped fresh herbs or a little chopped onion if you wish.

Pre-heat the oven to gas mark 7, 425°F (220°C), and light the grill. Put a little oil or dripping into a medium-sized roasting tin and place in the oven.

Prick the sausages all over and grill them to partly cook and lose some of their fat for 5–10 minutes, depending on their size and thickness. Take the hot roasting tin from the oven (the oil or dripping should by now be sizzling) and pour in about half of the batter mixture so that it sets very slightly. Quickly arrange the sausages and kidneys (if using) on the pudding and pour over the remaining batter. Cook in the oven for 30–40 minutes or until the pudding is puffed up and golden. Serve immediately.

Glazed gammon with Cumberland sauce

A gammon joint is always consumed with great relish; it is also inexpensive and easy to cook. I like it with a good parsley sauce, but Cumberland sauce is pretty well unbeatable. The important thing is to ask your butcher how much soaking the gammon will need and whether it is smoked or unsmoked – unsmoked gammon needs less, if any, soaking. Save the stock in which the gammon was cooked (if it is not too salty) for Ham, Parsley and Sweetcorn Pie (page 117) or for a ham and pea or bean soup.

Serves 6

3½–4 lb (1.65–1.8 kg) rolled middle-cut gammon joint

1 large onion, peeled, halved and stuck with a few cloves

1 large carrot, peeled and cut into chunks

1 stick celery, sliced

1 bay leaf

3 sprigs parsley

½ teaspoon black peppercorns

2–3 tablespoons dark brown sugar

1 tablespoon English mustard

About 30 cloves

5 fl oz (150 ml) dry cider

Cumberland Sauce:

2 oranges

2 lemons

1 lb (450 g) good-quality redcurrant jelly

10 fl oz (300 ml) port

1 tablespoon Grand Marnier (optional)

2 teaspoons arrowroot

2 teaspoons English mustard powder

Soak the gammon in water for a few hours or as recommended by your butcher (see the introduction to this recipe). Drain, then put in a large heavy saucepan, cover with water and bring to the boil. Skim, then add the onion, carrot, celery, bay leaf, parsley and peppercorns. Simmer for about 1 hour or roughly 15 minutes to the lb (450 g) – if this does not seem long, remember that the gammon will be cooked further in the oven after the initial boiling.

Remove the gammon from its stock; strain the stock and reserve it for another recipe. Pre-heat the oven to gas mark 5, 375°F (190°C). Peel the skin off the gammon joint and score the fat diagonally to make a diamond pattern. Rub about 2 tablespoons of the sugar and the mustard all over the fat, then stud each diamond with a clove. Put the ham into a roasting tin and bake in the oven for about 20 minutes. Pour over the cider, dredge with the remaining 1 tablespoon sugar, turn the oven down to gas mark 4, 350°F (180°C), and continue cooking without basting for a further 15–20 minutes.

Cumberland Sauce is served cold, so if possible make it the day before. Thinly pare the rind of 1 orange and 1 lemon, cut into matchsticks and blanch in boiling water for 5 minutes. Drain and refresh in cold water. Now place the redcurrant jelly, port and Grand Marnier (if using) in a saucepan, heat until just under simmering and cook very gently for about 5 minutes. Mix the arrowroot with 1 tablespoon cold water and stir into the pan until the mixture has thickened. Remove from the heat. Squeeze the juice of all the fruit (including the 2 you have peeled) into a bowl, add the blanched rind and stir in the mustard powder. Add the redcurrant mixture and combine well. Cool before serving with the gammon.

Flat plate bacon and egg pie

A simple main course, especially popular with children and useful to have in your repertoire when pondering uneasily in front of a somewhat bare refrigerator. It is a very quick dish to prepare as the bacon and eggs are not pre-cooked – they cook themselves in the pastry. Serve with jacket potatoes, grilled tomatoes and a crisp green salad.

Serves 4–6

A little butter for greasing

7 eggs

12 oz (350 g) shortcrust pastry, chilled

6–8 short back or lean streaky rashers bacon

Freshly ground black pepper

Worcestershire sauce

1 handful parsley, finely chopped

Pre-heat the oven to gas mark 6, 400°F (200°C).

Very lightly grease a large ovenproof plate with butter. Beat 1 of the eggs to use for glazing the pastry. Roll out half the pastry and line the plate with it. Brush the rim of the pastry with a little beaten egg or water. Cut the bacon into 3 inch (7.5 cm) long pieces and arrange them on the pastry base, leaving 6 gaps or hollows around the edge, just inside the rim of the pastry, into which you then carefully break the 6 remaining eggs. Season with lots of freshly ground black pepper and sprinkle well with Worcestershire sauce. Cover with the parsley. Roll out the remaining pastry and use to form a lid for the pie. Seal and trim the edge of the pie, making a little nick near the position of each egg to act as a guide when slicing and serving. Glaze the pie with beaten egg and bake in the oven for 10–15 minutes, then turn down the heat to gas mark 4, 350°F (180°C), and continue baking for a further 30 minutes. Serve warm.

Ham, parsley and sweetcorn pie

If you have about 1 lb (450 g) cooked gammon left over from a joint, try using it in this homely pie which is very good hot or cold. Alternatively, buy a gammon hock which is very cheap and gives succulent meat for casseroles or pies – and tasty stock. The pie is also delicious if, in place of the ham, you use cooked chicken and some chopped red or green pepper, or flaked cooked fish and 2 chopped hard-boiled eggs.

The pastry is an old-fashioned potato pastry – quite light and not too rich. When I make this sort of countryish pie with white-flour pastry, I often dredge the pastry board with wholemeal flour to give a rustic speckled appearance to the golden crust.

Serve with steamed spring greens or cabbage.

Serves 4–6

1 lb (450 g) cold cooked gammon, cut into bite-sized pieces

1 quantity Béchamel Sauce (page 217)

1 medium onion, peeled and finely chopped

A little gammon stock or white wine

Pinch of salt

Freshly ground black pepper

1–2 generous handfuls parsley, finely chopped

1 × 12 oz (350 g) tin sweetcorn, drained

1–1½ lb (450–700 g) cold cooked gammon, cut into bite-sized pieces

1 egg, beaten

Potato pastry:

½ teaspoon baking powder

4 oz (110 g) plain flour

2–3 oz (50–75 g) unsalted butter

8 oz (225 g) cold mashed potato

First make the pastry. Sift together the baking powder and flour and rub in the butter until the mixture resembles breadcrumbs. Mix in the mashed potato and (if necessary) enough chilled water to form a light unsticky dough. Knead lightly and briskly. Cover and chill for at least 1 hour.

Pre-heat the oven to gas mark 6, 400°F (200°C). Make the béchamel sauce, using less than the usual amount of milk: it needs to be very thick and of a binding consistency.

Meanwhile, simmer the onion in a little gammon stock or white wine for about 10 minutes or until soft, then add it with the stock or wine to the sauce. Taste and season with salt and pepper if necessary. Stir in the parsley and sweetcorn and cook through for 1–2 minutes. Add the ham, mix well, remove from the heat and allow to cool a little.

Roll out half the pastry to a thickness of about ¼ inch (6 mm) and use it to line a shallow pie-dish. Brush the edge with a little beaten egg. Tip in the ham filling. Roll out the rest of the pastry to form a lid and cover the pie with it. Seal and brush the pastry lid with beaten egg. Bake in the oven for 15 minutes, then turn down the heat to gas mark 4, 350°F (180°C), and continue cooking for a further 30 minutes.

Roasted or grilled pig's trotters

This is a classic delicacy in France, but not so well known in this country. Pig's trotters have gone rather out of fashion, although I remember eating them as a child. You can make quite a dish of them if you have time to remove the bones and fill them with a tasty stuffing; but they are also a good simple dish when plainly breadcrumbed and oven-baked or grilled. You need a fairly strongly flavoured sauce or relish for these trotters – a good pepped-up tartare sauce is excellent. Mashed potatoes or green lentils go well with them too.

You may find that during their long simmering the trotters become rather misshapen. Tying them firmly in several places with string or even binding them to conveniently sized flat pieces of wood will obviate this problem. However, I do not mind the slightly curled appearance of untrammelled trotters – it rather adds to the charm of the dish.

Serves 4

4 pig's trotters

Salt

1 large onion, peeled and quartered

2–3 carrots, peeled and sliced

2 sticks celery, sliced

1 bouquet garni (parsley, bay leaf, thyme)

1 strip lemon rind

Freshly ground black pepper

10 fl oz (300 ml) white wine

2–3 oz (50–70 g) butter, melted

About 8 oz (225 g) breadcrumbs made from day-old bread

Tartare sauce to serve

First rub the trotters all over with salt and leave them for a few hours or, preferably, overnight. Rinse off the salt and put the trotters into a large saucepan with the vegetables, bouquet garni and lemon rind. Season with just a pinch of salt and lots of freshly ground black pepper. Add the wine and top up with enough water to cover. Heat until barely simmering and simmer for at least 3 hours or until the meat is tender and beginning to fall away from the bones. Using 2 slotted spoons, carefully transfer the trotters to a plate and allow to cool. Strain the gelatinous stock and reserve it for another recipe.

When you are ready to finish the dish, pre-heat the oven to gas mark 7, 425°F (220°C). Carefully cut the trotters in half lengthways. Brush all over with the melted butter and roll in the breadcrumbs. Place on a baking sheet and roast in the oven for about 15 minutes or until the trotters are really hot and crisp.

Alternatively, if you have a good hot and efficient grill, the trotters may be grilled.

Serve immediately on warmed dinner plates and hand the tartare sauce separately.

Stuffed cabbage

There are countless variations of stuffed cabbage and, as is often the case, the simplest is the best. For this recipe you just pop the stuffing into the hollowed-out cabbage and cook it gently in stock or water with flavouring vegetables. Vegetarians could try various combinations of stuffing with nuts (especially chestnuts), rice, herbs, spices, raisins and so on. It is not the most picturesque dish in the world but no less delicious for that.

Serves 6

1 large white or Savoy cabbage

Pinch of salt

4 rashers green streaky bacon, de-rinded and chopped

1 onion, peeled and finely chopped

1½ lb (700 g) Lincolnshire sausages

4 oz (110 g) tinned chestnuts

Freshly ground black pepper

Fresh white breadcrumbs or cooked rice (for a very large cabbage)

Sauce (optional):

2–3 carrots, peeled and sliced

1 turnip, peeled and sliced

1 onion, peeled and sliced

1 stick celery, sliced

1 ham bone

A little French mustard

1 egg yolk or a little cream

Working from the base, use a sharp knife to remove the stem and core of the cabbage. Then use a strong spoon to scoop out more of the centre, leaving a wall about 1 inch (2.5 cm) thick. Blanch the cabbage in a large pan of gently boiling salted water for a few minutes to soften the leaves a little. Drain well, reserving the water, and remove and reserve 2 or 3 of the outer leaves.

In a heavy frying-pan gently fry the bacon until the fat runs, then remove it with a slotted spoon and put into a mixing bowl. Add the onion to the fat in the pan and fry until soft but not brown. Skin the sausages and cut them into small pieces. Add the sausages, onion and chestnuts to the bacon and season with a small amount of salt and freshly ground black pepper (Lincolnshire sausages are usually well seasoned). Put this mixture into the hollowed-out cabbage. (If the cabbage is very large, you may need to expand the stuffing with some fresh white breadcrumbs or cooked rice.) Cover the opening in the cabbage with the reserved leaves and tie up with 2 lengths of kitchen string. Put the cabbage into a large heavy saucepan or flameproof casserole and pour in enough of the reserved cabbage cooking water almost to cover. Add a few sliced carrots and a sliced turnip, onion and celery stick to the water if you wish – or a ham bone if there is room. Cover the pan with a lid and cook very slowly at barely simmering point for at least 2½–3 hours. The cabbage should be totally tender: test it with a skewer or knitting needle.

Serve hot or warm, cut into wedges like a cake, with some of the reduced cooking liquid poured over. This liquid can be pepped up with a little mustard and thickened with an egg yolk or cream if you like, but as it stands it is very delicious indeed.

Ham, sausage and cabbage soup with cheese scones

Cabbage and pork are a super combination, and here they are used in a rustic and beautifully flavoured family main course soup which is really more of a stew. Look for locally produced smoked ham (see page 27 for information on ham) – you could buy scraps – and spicy Italian sausages or Frankfurters. If you do not eat meat, make this soup with vegetable stock and add some sliced runner beans near the end of the cooking time. Served with the fresh warm cheese scones (or with toasted cheese on floating slices of French bread if you prefer), this is a wonderfully heartening winter's supper.

Serves 4–6

1 medium white cabbage, stalk removed and chopped or shredded

1–2 oz (25–50 g) unsalted butter

1 large onion, peeled and chopped

2–3 fat cloves garlic, peeled and chopped

2½ pints (1.4 litres) home-made vegetable or clear chicken stock

Pinch of salt

Freshly ground black pepper

8 oz (225 g) chunks or scraps of cooked ham

4–6 good-quality sausages, cut into chunks

Cheese Scones:

1 oz (25 g) butter

8 oz (225 g) self-raising flour

Pinch of salt

2 teaspoons baking powder

2–3 oz (50–75 g) Cheddar cheese, grated

5 fl oz (150 ml) milk and water (50:50 mixture)

Milk to glaze

First blanch the cabbage in boiling water for a few seconds and drain well.

In a large heavy-bottomed saucepan or flameproof casserole, melt the butter and gently cook the onion and garlic until soft but not brown. Add the cabbage and stir well until glistening, then pour over the stock. Season with salt and pepper according to how well the stock is seasoned, heat until simmering and cook gently for about 1 hour. Add the ham and sausage pieces and continue simmering for a further hour. Add more stock if necessary.

Meanwhile, make the scones. Pre-heat the oven to gas mark 7, 425°F (220°C), 30 minutes before you are due to eat. Rub the butter into the sifted flour, salt and baking powder. Then mix in the cheese. Make a well in the centre of the mixture, pour in the milk and water and use a knife to draw in the sides to form a light non-sticky dough. Pat this dough out on a floured work-surface to a thickness of ¾ inch (2 cm) and use a cutter to cut out the scones. Place them on a baking sheet, brush with a little milk and bake near the top of the oven for about 12 minutes or until well risen and golden. Serve warm with the soup.

Poultry
and
Eggs

Tarragon roast chicken with almond sauce

Make sure that you have a fresh chicken that promises to have some flavour, and try to find some fresh French tarragon which has far more flavour than the Russian variety. This is a simple recipe; and, if you wish, the sauce can be prepared in advance and gently re-heated.

Serves 6

3½–4 lb (1.65–1.8 kg) fresh roasting chicken

4 sprigs tarragon, plus a few leaves to garnish

2 oz (50 g) butter

3 oz (75 g) almonds, ground or very finely chopped

10 fl oz (300 ml) chicken stock

Pinch each of salt, sugar and mace

3 tablespoons single cream

Pre-heat the oven to gas mark 6, 400°F (200°C). Wash the chicken inside and out and pat dry. Remove any visible fat from the cavity and push in a sprig of tarragon and a little nut of butter. Rub some softened butter all over the bird and lay it in the middle of a large sheet of thick aluminium foil. Tuck some tarragon in the fold between each leg and breast, put a sprig on top of the breast and parcel up the chicken loosely but securely. Put the bird in a roasting tin on its side and roast in the oven for about 30 minutes. Then turn it on to its other side and roast for a further 30 minutes. Now lay it on its back, peel back the foil and roast it for the final 30–40 minutes, basting occasionally – you should allow a total cooking time of approximately 20 minutes to the lb (450 g) plus 20 minutes extra. To test whether the chicken is done, gently wiggle one of the legs, which should 'give' easily; peer into the cavity to check the juices, which should be clear and not pink. Let the chicken rest in a warm place for 15 minutes before carving.

While the chicken is roasting, make the sauce. In a heavy frying-pan, melt a nut of butter and gently fry the almonds in it, stirring all the time, until they are golden-brown. Add the chicken stock and salt, sugar and mace to taste and simmer for 5 minutes. Stir in the cream and cook gently without boiling for 3–4 more minutes.

To serve, carve the chicken and arrange on warmed dinner plates. Pour the sauce over the slices and garnish with a few single tarragon leaves.

Aromatic roast chicken and fennel

My favourite cooking vessel for chicken is an inexpensive large oval enamel dish with a dimpled lid. With the addition of liquid – wine and/or stock – you can achieve a succulent combination of tender poached meat with a crispy roasted surface. Here is a fragrant recipe based on my standard everyday way of cooking a family chicken. Serve with rice or potatoes, and follow with a green salad.

Serves 6

4 lb (1.8 kg) fresh roasting chicken (with giblets if possible)

1 lb (450 g) bulbs fennel, trimmed and quartered, green fronds reserved

1½ pints (900 ml) light chicken or vegetable stock

1–2 tablespoons Pernod or Ricard

6 green cardamom pods, split and seeds crushed slightly

2 teaspoons crushed coriander seeds

2 cloves garlic, peeled

1 inch (2.5 cm) cube fresh root ginger, peeled and sliced

Pinch of salt

Freshly ground black pepper

A little sunflower oil

Pre-heat the oven to gas mark 6, 400°F (200°C).

Wash the chicken inside and out under running water and thoroughly pat dry with kitchen paper. Cut out and discard any visible fat. The chicken should be allowed to come up to room temperature before cooking.

In a large shallow pan covered with a lid, gently simmer the fennel in 15 fl oz (400 ml) of the stock with the Pernod or Ricard for about 10–15 minutes. Remove the fennel with a slotted spoon and stuff into the chicken cavity – push some into the neck end too. Use wooden skewers to secure the openings. Place the chicken in a lidded braising dish – it should be a nice tight fit; if not, you should truss the chicken (see page 34). Pour in the fennel cooking liquid and add more stock until the liquid comes half-way up the chicken. If you have the chicken giblets, push these in around the bird with the cardamom, coriander, garlic and ginger. Season the chicken lightly with salt and pepper, trickle just a little oil over the breast, and clamp the lid on the dish. Cook in the oven for about 1¾ hours or until cooked through (see page 36 for how to test for this). You should allow a cooking time of about 20 minutes to the lb (450 g) plus 20 minutes extra.

Using 2 spatulas transfer the roast chicken to a warmed serving platter and keep warm. Strain the cooking liquid into a bowl and cool somewhat. Use kitchen paper to blot off all the fat that has risen to the surface. Strain the liquid again into a saucepan and – depending on how much the liquid has already reduced – add a little more of the remaining stock. Also add the juices which will have seeped from the cooked chicken. Boil the liquid rapidly to reduce it somewhat and intensify the flavour. Taste it and adjust the seasoning if necessary, adding a dash more Pernod or Ricard if you wish. The result should be a clear, thinnish, fragrant sauce to which a professional chef might add cubes of butter or a dash of cream to finish; I prefer it to be light and clear. When carving the chicken, use a spoon to retrieve the beautiful moist quarters of fennel from inside the bird: these can be served with the dish which should be garnished with the reserved green fennel fronds.

Corn-fed chicken with 40 cloves of garlic

This aromatic dish is easy to prepare and ideal for a relaxed and informal supper party. The whole unpeeled cloves of garlic are meltingly transformed as they roast alongside the chicken – soft and curiously sweet. If you cannot find a corn-fed chicken, use a fresh free-range young roasting bird. Serve with lots of green salad and a casserole of potatoes, baked jacket potatoes or very fresh warm bread.

Serves 4

3 lb (1.4 kg) fresh corn-fed roasting chicken

Pinch of salt

Freshly ground black pepper

3–4 sprigs fresh rosemary

40 cloves garlic

1 small lemon, quartered

About 6 tablespoons good-quality olive oil

Pre-heat the oven to gas mark 6, 400°F (200°C).
Rinse the bird inside and out under running water and pat dry thoroughly with kitchen paper. Trim away any visible fat, season the inside of the bird, tuck in 1–2 sprigs bruised rosemary, 3–4 unpeeled garlic cloves and the

lemon quarters (give them a little squeeze to release a sprinkling of juice). Truss the chicken (see page 34) and place it in a baking dish into which it fits snugly (as described in the recipe for Aromatic Roast Chicken and Fennel, page 125). Surround it with the remaining unpeeled garlic cloves and 1–2 sprigs rosemary and trickle the oil all over the chicken and garlic. Cook in the oven, uncovered, for 15 minutes. Then baste the breast with the oil, turn the oven down to gas mark 4, 350°F (180°C), and cook for a further hour or until done (see page 36 for how to test for this) – allow about 20 minutes to the lb (450 g) plus 20 minutes extra.

Now, using 2 spatulas, carefully lift the chicken from the dish, set it on a warmed serving platter, cover with aluminium foil and let it rest in a warm place for 15 minutes before carving.

Serve the chicken surrounded by the soft cloves of garlic. Your guests use their fingers to split open the cloves, which can be spread on to a hunk of bread or piece of potato and consumed with great relish along with the scented pieces of chicken and its juices.

Herbed poussins

A summery supper party dish to linger over – and most of the preparation can be done in advance. Do use fresh herbs, and serve with plenty of steamed baby vegetables and tiny new potatoes.

Serves 4

4 poussins

1 tablespoon each finely chopped fresh parsley, thyme and marjoram or oregano or tarragon

1 lemon, quartered

4–8 cloves garlic (depending on size)

Pinch of salt

Freshly ground black pepper

Good-quality olive oil

Rinse the poussins and pat dry with kitchen paper. Untruss them and, working from the neck end of each bird, very gently ease the skin away from the breast without breaking or tearing it. Smother the breasts under the skin with the herbs and press the skin back down. Slip a lemon quarter and 1–2 unpeeled garlic cloves into the cavity of each bird. This preparation can be done in advance and the poussins refrigerated until you are ready to cook, but remember to bring them back up to room temperature before roasting.

Pre-heat the oven to gas mark 5, 375°F (190°C). Put the poussins into a deep roasting tin, sprinkle with a little salt and pepper, and drizzle olive oil over the birds. Do this with a light touch: the oil should just annoint the poussins and barely cover the base of the roasting tin. Cover the tin very loosely with aluminium foil and cook in the oven for about 30 minutes. Remove the foil and continue cooking for a further 15 minutes to brown the birds. Make sure that they are done by using the test described on page 36.

To serve, the poussins can be presented as they are or split in two, set on warmed plates with a flourish of vegetables.

Risotto with chicken livers and fennel

A beautiful creamy dish of rice and fennel, topped with chicken livers with a hint of garlic, and strewn with chopped green fennel leaves.

Serves 4–6

8 oz (225 g) chicken livers

4 tablespoons olive oil

2 medium onions, peeled and finely chopped

2 bulbs fennel, trimmed and coarsely chopped, green fronds reserved

1 bay leaf

2–3 parsley stalks, bruised

3 cloves garlic, peeled

14 oz (400 g) Arborio (Italian risotto) rice

About 2½ pints (1.4 litres) home-made chicken stock

Pinch of salt

Freshly ground black pepper

A little butter (optional)

First trim and rinse the chicken livers, pat dry with kitchen paper and set aside.

Heat 2 tablespoons of the oil in a large heavy-bottomed pan and gently cook the onions in it without browning for about 5 minutes. Now add the fennel, bay leaf, parsley stalks and 2 of the whole garlic cloves, stir well and continue to cook gently for a further 2 minutes. Add the rice and stir again until all the rice is coated with the oil and well combined with the onions – add a little more oil at this stage if necessary.

Meanwhile, heat the stock and, when it is scarcely simmering, pour enough into the rice just to cover it. Stir gently. As the rice absorbs the stock, add more – a cup or ladleful at a time – and continue cooking and stirring for about 20 minutes or until the rice is *al dente* – that is, neither crunchy nor mushy and soft. The last ladleful of stock should not be totally absorbed, so that the risotto has a liquid, creamy, sauce-like consistency. Remove the bay leaf, garlic cloves and parsley stalks and discard. Check the seasoning and add a little salt and pepper if necessary. The risotto can be covered and kept warm for 5 minutes with a nut of butter on top.

Now heat the 2 remaining tablespoons oil in a heavy frying-pan and throw in the prepared livers. Cook them evenly on both sides over a moderate heat for 3–5 minutes, adding the remaining garlic clove, finely chopped, half-way through the cooking time. The livers are ready when no more blood appears on their surface and they have become firm but still have a slightly rosy interior.

Chop the reserved green fennel fronds. Transfer the risotto to a large, shallow, warmed serving dish, cover with the livers and scatter over a handful or two of the chopped fennel fronds. Serve immediately.

Poached chicken with aïoli sauce

Although this recipe is extremely simple, I am explaining it in fairly minute detail because it contains a good blueprint method of cooking chicken which unfailingly produces a tender, succulent and virtually fat-free bird together with a flavoursome stock. The chicken is elegantly served in shallow soup bowls with slices of potato and a vegetable garnish and strewn with chopped parsley – rather in the manner of the classic fish soup, la bourride – *and your guests will need a knife, fork and spoon with which to eat it. Aïoli is a strong garlic-flavoured mayonnaise, here combined with stock to make a tingling sauce. It is very delicious indeed.*

Serves 4

3–4 lb (1.4–1.8 kg) fresh roasting chicken

1 large onion, peeled and quartered

2 leeks, trimmed and sliced

1 carrot, peeled and sliced

1–2 sticks celery, sliced

1 bunch herbs (bay leaf, parsley, thyme)

1 strip orange rind

4–5 ripe tomatoes, skinned, de-seeded and chopped

Pinch of salt

About 10 peppercorns, crushed

10 fl oz (300 ml) dry white wine

1 quantity Aïoli (see page 215)

Chopped parsley to garnish

To serve:

4 potatoes

A *julienne* of carrots

A *julienne* of baby turnips   } as available

A *julienne* of celeriac or Jerusalem artichokes

1 small bulb fennel, finely sliced

Rinse the chicken and pat it dry with kitchen paper. Put it into a flameproof casserole or heavy saucepan of a size which fits it fairly tightly. Surround the bird with the onion, leeks, carrot, celery, herbs, orange rind, tomatoes and seasoning. Pour in the wine and add water to just about cover the chicken. Bring to the boil, let the liquid bubble once or twice, turn down the heat until the liquid is barely simmering, skim if necessary and poach the bird for about 1–1¼ hours or until thoroughly cooked (see page 36 for how to test for this).

While the chicken is simmering, prepare the Aïoli and have it ready in a small saucepan.

Using 2 slotted spoons, carefully lift the chicken out of its cooking liquid and set it on a warmed plate. Take off the breasts, thighs and back meat, remove the skin from all these pieces and reserve it. Cover the chicken meat and keep it warm. Break up the carcass and return it with the skin to the poaching liquid. Boil fiercely until the liquid is reduced by half. Strain into a jug, cool quickly and, using first a spoon then absorbent kitchen paper, skim and blot off all the fat.

Pour a little of this stock into the prepared Aïoli over a very low heat, stirring continuously with a wooden spoon or wire whisk. Continue adding the stock, stirring all the time until you have achieved a thinnish yet creamy sauce – taste as you go. Remove the sauce from the heat and keep warm.

Boil, drain and slice the potatoes. Steam all the other vegetables. Keep the vegetables warm.

To serve, slice the poached chicken into attractive manageable pieces and divide them with the slices of potato between 4 warmed shallow soup bowls. Scatter over the steamed vegetables and pour over the gently re-heated Aïoli Sauce. Dust with the chopped parsley and serve immediately.

Peppery grilled chicken with lemon

Serve with a large bowl of warm potatoes and chopped red onions dressed with vinaigrette, a green salad and extra wedges of lemon for squeezing.

Serves 6

6 fresh chicken wings

6 fresh chicken drumsticks

2 lemons, thinly sliced, plus lemon wedges to serve (optional)

6 cloves garlic, peeled and crushed

6 tablespoons good-quality olive oil

1 tablespoon lightly crushed black peppercorns

½ tablespoon lightly crushed coriander seeds

Wipe the chicken with dampened kitchen paper and pat dry. Using a sharp knife, make a few small cuts in each wing and drumstick. In a glass or earthenware bowl large enough to hold all the chicken, mix together the lemon slices, garlic, olive oil, crushed peppercorns and coriander, then add the chicken pieces, smothering them well. Leave covered in a cool place for 6 hours, turning occasionally.

When you are ready to cook, pre-heat the grill until it is good and hot. Oil the grill rack and heat this until it is very hot also. Lift the chicken pieces out of their marinade, giving them a shake as you do so. Put the first 6 pieces on the red-hot grill rack in order to make attractive brand marks on the skin. Turn the grill down to moderate and grill the chicken pieces for about 5 minutes on each side for wings and 6 minutes on each side for drumsticks or until cooked through. Baste occasionally with the marinade. Keep the first batch of chicken pieces warm while you grill the second batch in exactly the same way. Serve immediately with lemon wedges to squeeze over the chicken if you wish.

Thyme-scented steamed chicken breasts with four vegetables

What I love about this light delectable little main course is that it is so easy to cook just for one or two or, if you have a large enough steamer, for three or four people. And the preparation takes only minutes if you have previously prepared the Fresh Tomato Sauce. Chicken breasts can be rather dry, but this cooking method, together with the creamy stuffing, gives succulent results – and you can use a low-fat cream cheese if you wish. Eat the chicken straight from the parcel set on a plate – on a tray on your knee if you like – with perhaps some plain boiled potatoes and a crisp green salad.

Serves 2

A little sunflower oil

2–3 sprigs fresh thyme

4 oz (110 g) cream cheese or ricotta

2 fresh chicken breasts, skinned and boned

1 carrot, cut into *julienne* strips

1 stick celery, cut into *julienne* strips

1 leek or 2 spring onions, cut into *julienne* strips

2 oz (50 g) turnip, cut into *julienne* strips

Pinch of salt

Freshly ground black pepper

A little dry white wine

1 quantity Fresh Tomato Sauce (see page 214) to serve

First set up the steamer. Cut out 2 double-thickness rounds of aluminium foil, each large enough to make a generous parcel of 1 chicken breast, and oil them very lightly.

Lightly crush about 1 teaspoon of the thyme leaves and fork into the cheese. Wipe the chicken breasts with dampened kitchen paper and pat dry. Use a sharp knife to slice open a long pocket in the side of each breast and fill with the cheese and a little more of the crushed thyme. Place a breast in the centre of each foil circle and surround with neat separate bundles of each prepared vegetable. Season the chicken and vegetables with salt and pepper, splash a little wine over each breast and place a whole sprig of bruised thyme on the top. Bring up the sides of the parcel to crimp so that you form a crescent shape rather like a Cornish pasty. Crimp loosely but securely, place in the steamer basket and steam for 25–30 minutes or until the chicken is cooked through. Towards the end of the cooking time re-heat the Fresh Tomato Sauce.

To serve, put the parcels on warm plates, open to release a warm thyme-scented rush of delight, remove the thyme sprig and spoon over a small helping of warm Fresh Tomato Sauce. Alternatively, lift the chicken and vegetables out of the parcel and arrange on warmed plates, add the cooking juices in the parcels to the sauce, heat through and reduce a little if necessary before pouring over the dish.

Tropical chicken with lime and rum

This is a spicy one-pot dish, a sort of tropical pilaff, which I have adapted from
Caribbean Cooking *by Elisabeth Lambert Ortiz. Angostura bitters – the flavouring
that makes pink gin pink and is also used in fruit and ice-cream dishes – is a West Indian
flavouring and well worth acquiring for your store-cupboard.*

Serves 4–6

3 lb (1.4 kg) fresh chicken pieces

3–4 tablespoons olive oil

1 onion, peeled and finely chopped

2–3 fat cloves garlic, peeled and finely chopped

2 fresh green chillies, de-seeded and finely chopped

1 green pepper, de-seeded and finely chopped

12 oz (350 g) rice

1 sachet saffron powder or 2–3 pinches of saffron threads

Juice of 1 lime and 1 strip of rind

About 1 pint (570 ml) chicken stock

¼ teaspoon Angostura bitters

Pinch of salt

Freshly ground black pepper

3–4 tablespoons white rum

Wipe the chicken pieces with dampened kitchen paper, pat dry and trim off
any fat. If they are large, divide into smaller pieces. In a large heavy frying-
pan heat 2 tablespoons of the olive oil and brown the chicken all over. Using
a slotted spoon, transfer the pieces to a lidded flameproof casserole.

Add the remaining 1–2 tablespoons oil to the frying-pan and very gently
fry the onion, garlic, chillies and green pepper in it for a few minutes, taking
care not to brown them. Then add the rice and stir well until all the grains
are coated and glistening. Add the contents of the frying-pan to the chicken
in the casserole along with the saffron, lime juice and rind, chicken stock and
Angostura bitters. Season with a little salt and pepper. Heat until barely
simmering, cover and continue cooking on top of the stove for about 30
minutes or until the chicken and rice are cooked and most of the liquid
absorbed. Add the rum and cook, uncovered, for a further 3–4 minutes.

Pan-fried chicken breasts with papaya purée

Papaya (or paw paw) contains an enzyme which has a tenderising effect on meat and is much used for this purpose in the tropics – apart from which it is a wonderful fresh-tasting accompaniment to pork, fish and poultry. This is a simple main-course dish, picturesque on the plate and refreshingly light.

Serves 4

2 papayas

3 tablespoons fromage frais

2–3 tablespoons dry sherry

Pinch of salt

Freshly ground black pepper

Lemon juice

4 fresh chicken breasts, skinned and boned

A little flour

Pinch of ground ginger

½ oz (10 g) butter

First prepare the purée. Peel the papayas, cut them in half lengthways and scoop out the seeds. Cut the flesh into chunks, place in the bowl of a food processor or liquidiser together with the fromage frais and whizz until smooth. Add the sherry, a little salt and pepper and a good squeeze of lemon juice (or to taste). Pour the purée into a saucepan and heat very gently, at just under simmering point, for a few minutes, then taste and add a dash more lemon juice or sherry if necessary. Keep warm.

Wipe the chicken with dampened kitchen paper and pat dry. Season the flour with a pinch of salt, a little pepper and the ground ginger and dust the chicken breasts with it. Heat the butter in a heavy non-stick frying-pan and fry the chicken breasts in it over a moderate heat for about 6–8 minutes on each side or until cooked through. Towards the end of the cooking time, sprinkle in a little lemon juice.

Lift the breasts from the pan and serve each one on a pool of the papaya purée poured on to a warmed plate. If you like, you can slice each breast lengthways and arrange it in a fan shape.

Christmas turkey

If you are in a hurry to produce a Christmas turkey with a beautiful gravy, I am sure you will be in very good company. The holiday countdown is daunting, and every Christmastime there is a flurry of definitive turkey recipes in the magazines and colour supplements. One turkey producer even has a 24-hour turkey panic telephone hotline.

The first step towards the perfect turkey dinner is to order – well in advance of Christmas – a fresh free-range turkey: the flavour of a free-range bird is truly unbeatable. Hen birds of 8–12 lb (3.5–5.5 kg) are generally the best as regards taste and texture. A turkey of this size will feed an average family with enough left over to eat cold next day. Second, cook it by the semi-braised roasting method given below, using the giblets and neck for the braising liquid: turkey does tend to dryness and uneven cooking, but this method produces tender succulent flesh with a crisp-roasted surface.

If you have time, make stock by simmering the giblets with vegetables as described in the recipe for Roast Duckling on page 140, but cook them in this instance for 2 hours. Alternatively, add the giblets and vegetables to the liquid in the roasting tin which will also produce a flavoursome stock as the turkey cooks.

When you are ready to cook the turkey, pre-heat the oven to gas mark 4, 350°F (180°C). Wipe the bird inside and out with dampened kitchen paper and pat dry. Lift the skin at the neck end and, using a small sharp knife, carefully remove the wishbone: this will make carving the breast much easier. Stuff the neck end and cavity with your preferred stuffing. Weigh the bird and calculate the cooking time: you should allow approximately 20 minutes to the lb (450 g) plus an extra 20 minutes. Do not be tempted to cook the turkey at a higher heat than that recommended – it will shrink and become tough. Rub the breast and legs with a little butter or brush with oil and set the turkey in a roasting tin. Pour in at least 1 pint (570 ml) of the hot giblet stock – or, if you have not had time to make stock, the same amount of hot water to which you then add the giblets, some herbs, a peeled and chopped carrot and onion and some seasoning. Cover the breast with buttered greaseproof paper and foil and place in the oven.

Now proceed as follows. If you are cooking, say, a 9 lb (4 kg) turkey, roast it first for 1 hour. Then remove the butter paper and foil, turn the bird on its side and cook for another 40 minutes. Turn again on to its other side, and cook for a further 40 minutes. Add more hot stock or water to the roasting tin if necessary to keep the liquid to about 1 pint (570 ml). Finally, put the turkey on its back, remove the foil and cook for a further hour, basting occasionally. This gives a total cooking time of about 3 hours 20 minutes for a 9 lb (4 kg) bird; adjust the cooking time accordingly for a turkey of a different size.

Now carefully lift the bird from the roasting tin and set it on a warmed serving platter. Leave it to rest in a warm place for 15 minutes or so before carving.

Meanwhile, pour the stock into a basin, cool quickly and, using first a spoon and then absorbent kitchen paper, skim and blot off all the fat. Return the stock to a saucepan to re-heat, and either boil hard to reduce and thicken somewhat or thicken with *beurre manié* made with 1 oz (25 g) each of butter and flour (see page 16).

Deep-dish turkey pie

The eternal problem of turkey left-overs! Gratins, croquettes, sandwiches and soups are all good options. If you have about 2 lb (900 g) left-over cooked turkey, you might like to try this handsome pie. It is possible that you may also have some left-over stuffing, gravy and cooked potatoes which could be added to the filling to save on preparation time. Chunks of cooked parsnip or turnip may be used instead of potato if you wish, and sliced cooked sausages substituted for the forcemeat or stuffing balls. It is the well-flavoured sauce that makes this pie so good.

Serves 6

1 lb (450 g) shortcrust pastry

6 oz (175 g) mushrooms, wiped and thickly sliced

½ oz (10 g) butter

2 lb (900 g) cooked turkey pieces

About 10 forcemeat or stuffing balls (chestnut or walnut stuffing is particularly good)

8 oz (225 g) frozen peas, thawed and drained

1 lb (450 g) cooked potatoes, cubed

Beaten egg to glaze

Sauce:

1 small onion, peeled and finely chopped

1½ oz (40 g) butter

1½ oz (40 g) flour

10 fl oz (300 ml) hot milk

½ glass white wine

4–6 tablespoons giblet stock

Pinch of salt

Freshly ground black pepper

½ tablespoon finely chopped parsley

¼ teaspoon dried oregano or marjoram

First make the pastry, cover and chill for 1 hour.

Pre-heat the oven to gas mark 6, 400°F (200°C).

Meanwhile, make the sauce. In a heavy-bottomed saucepan, gently cook the onion in the butter for a few minutes until it is soft but not brown. Sprinkle in the flour and cook for a further 1–2 minutes without browning. Remove from the heat, add the hot milk and whisk or beat in to make a smooth sauce, then stir in the wine, stock, seasoning and herbs. Return to a low heat and simmer gently, stirring all the time, for 10 minutes. You should have a medium-thick sauce by now, but add a little more stock if necessary. Check the seasoning and set aside.

In a small saucepan, gently fry the mushrooms in the butter for a few minutes, then set aside.

Roll out half the pastry and use it to line the base of a pie-dish about 9 inches (23 cm) wide and 1½–2 inches (3–5 cm) deep, allowing a generous overlap around the rim of the dish. Fill the pie with the pieces of turkey, balls of forcemeat or stuffing, peas, potato cubes, mushrooms and their juices, and pour the sauce all over, giving it time to settle around the other ingredients. Brush the rim of the pastry with water or beaten egg. Then roll out the rest of the pastry to make a lid and cover the pie with it. Seal the edge, trim, and fork or thumb in a decorative border. Use a small knife to make a few slits in the centre of the lid, brush with beaten egg and bake in the oven for 15 minutes. Then turn the heat down to gas mark 4, 350°F (180°C), and cook for a further 40 minutes. Serve hot or cold.

Guinea fowl braised in cider with walnut, celery and apple stuffing

For those who find pheasant too gamy, guinea fowl is an excellent option – the flavour is somewhere between pheasant and chicken, and the bird is very lean. This is an easy recipe (which is, in fact, also suitable for pheasant), and is good served with cauliflower and Brussels sprouts.

Serves 4–6

2 guinea fowl (with giblets if possible)

3–4 tablespoons olive oil

2 leeks, trimmed and finely sliced

2 carrots, peeled and diced

2 sticks celery, sliced

½ medium onion, peeled and finely chopped

About ½ bottle Normandy or other dry cider

1–2 tablespoons single cream (optional)

A little arrowroot, cornflour or *beurre manié* (see page 16; optional)

Stuffing:

8 oz (225 g) white or wholemeal breadcrumbs

4 oz (110 g) walnuts, chopped or ground

4 oz (110 g) celery, finely chopped

½ onion, peeled and very finely chopped

1 apple, peeled and very finely chopped

1–2 teaspoons dried sage

2 eggs, beaten

Pinch of salt

Freshly ground black pepper

A little cider to moisten (optional)

Butter for greasing

Pre-heat the oven to gas mark 3, 325°F (170°C). Rinse the birds and pat dry with kitchen paper.

Combine the stuffing ingredients, moistening with a little cider if necessary. Put the mixture into a lightly buttered baking dish and cover with lightly buttered greaseproof paper.

In a large frying-pan heat the olive oil and brown the birds all over. Remove them, then brown all the vegetables. Drain the vegetables, put them in the bottom of a large roasting tin or baking dish and lay the birds on their sides on top, together with the giblets if using. Heat the cider and pour it in – it should be about 1½–2 inches (3–5 cm) deep. Put the dish of stuffing and the roasting tin containing the birds into the oven and cook for about 1½ hours, turning the birds to their other side half-way through this time.

Turn off the oven, remove the roasting tin and transfer the birds to a warm serving plate. Return to the oven to keep warm with the stuffing. Strain the stock from the roasting tin into a bowl and cool as quickly as possible (see page 12). Using a spoon followed by kitchen paper, skim and blot the fat from the surface. Re-heat the stock and reduce until thickened, stirring in the cream if using. (If you wish you can thicken it further with a little arrowroot, cornflour or *beurre manié* – see page 16 – though I prefer it as it is.) If the vegetables from the stock look respectable, they can be re-heated to serve with the dish.

Carve the birds in the same way as for chicken and serve on warmed plates with slices of stuffing and a little of the gravy poured over.

Roast duckling

This slow-roasting method produces a succulent fine-tasting dish. The duckling breasts are served with button onions and baby turnips glazed in stock with a marvellous gravy and green lentils, though creamed potatoes and carrots are also good with this roast. The following day strips of the remaining duck may be transformed into a warm salad with an orange dressing and garnished with duck cracklings (page 143), or can be tossed with reserved stock in a bowl of steaming pasta. You will be left with a good quantity of duck fat which can be used to give flavour to roast or sautéed potatoes and other vegetables, and to meat when searing it for casseroles. I was surprised to learn that poultry fat contains 9 per cent cholesterol compared with butter's 22 per cent. Far less poultry fat is required than oil or butter when frying, and it will store in the refrigerator for several weeks or may be frozen.

Serves 4

5½–6 lb (2.5–2.75 kg) ducklings (with giblets)

1 small onion, peeled and finely chopped

2 carrots, peeled and diced

2 sticks celery, sliced

1 piece turnip, peeled and diced

1 bunch herbs (parsley, thyme, bay leaf)

1 glass red wine

Freshly ground black pepper

To serve:

12 oz (350 g) green lentils

20 button onions, peeled

Pinch of sugar (optional)

6 baby turnips, peeled and sliced into thin rounds

Pinch of salt

First wash the ducklings, pat them dry thoroughly inside and out with kitchen paper and leave them in a cool airy place for a few hours so that they become as dry as possible.

Pre-heat the oven to gas mark 7, 425°F (220°C). Prick the skin of the ducklings all over with a fork or skewer – deeply enough to ensure that the fat can escape but take care not to puncture the lean flesh. Set the ducklings on a rack over a roasting tin and roast in the oven for 30 minutes. Then turn down the heat to gas mark 4, 350°F (180°C), and continue cooking for another 30 minutes. Take the tin from the oven, set the birds aside on a warm plate, remove the rack from the tin and pour all the fat into a bowl. (There will be up to 1 pint (570 ml) clear duck fat.) Return the ducklings to the roasting tin – *without* the rack this time – and put them back in the oven.

Now make the stock. In a heavy-bottomed saucepan heat ½ tablespoon of the reserved duck fat and sweat the chopped and sliced vegetables until they are soft but not brown. Add the herbs, duckling giblets, wine and pepper and enough water to cover. Simmer for 1 hour. Then take the ducklings from the oven again, pour off any fat from the roasting tin, then pour all the strained stock over the ducklings and continue cooking them for a final hour or so, basting occasionally with the stock.

Remove the ducklings from the oven and cut off the 4 breast sections. Set aside the rest of the ducklings for later use. Remove the skin from the breasts and reserve – this will make cracklings for use in another meal. Turn off the oven, put the breasts on a warm plate and keep warm in the warm oven. Pour the stock into a bowl and cool it very quickly (see page 12). Using a spoon first and then kitchen paper, skim and blot off any fat that has risen to the surface of the stock.

Meanwhile cook the lentils in the usual way. Then, in a heavy-bottomed pan, cover the button onions in a little of the stock and simmer for about 10 minutes, turning up the heat and boiling hard for a few seconds at the end to reduce the stock to about 1 tablespoon. Add a pinch of sugar at this stage if you wish. Do the same with the turnips in another pan. To make the gravy, reduce the remaining stock somewhat. Add salt to taste.

Slice the duck breasts, arrange on warmed dinner plates with the onions, turnips and lentils. Pour over a little gravy and serve. Hand the remaining gravy in a jug.

Simple duck breasts with apple sauce

You can buy prepared duck breasts or, alternatively, cut the breasts off two duckling portions and use the remaining bones to make a quick stock for a simple gravy or for use in another recipe.

The breasts are cooked very briefly so that they are rare, and I serve them with a simple apple sauce flavoured with a good squeeze of lemon juice and a dash of crème de cassis. The whole operation takes less than 30 minutes. Steamed young green beans and a potato gratin are good accompaniments.

Serves 2

1 quantity Apple Sauce (see page 109)

Juice of ½ lemon

Dash of crème de cassis

Pinch of salt

Freshly ground pepper

2 duck breasts

First prepare the Apple Sauce. Add lemon juice, crème de cassis and seasoning to taste and keep warm.

Wipe the duck breasts with dampened kitchen paper and pat dry. Heat a frying-pan or wok (non-stick if possible) and, when it is really hot, put in the duck breasts, skin side down, and fry for about 3 minutes. The skin will release plenty of fat. Turn the breasts over and continue frying for 6–7 minutes or until they are just beginning to lose their pinkness.

To serve, either leave the fat on the duck breasts or remove it. Slice each breast across the grain and fan the slices out on 2 warmed dinner plates. Alternatively, thinly slice the breasts lengthways and fan out in the same way. Spoon some of the sauce alongside and serve immediately.

A warm salad of duck with orange dressing and cracklings

For this wonderful salad use the roast duckling meat remaining after you have removed the breast sections from the carcasses for the recipe on page 140. Serve with plenty of crusty bread or a warm potato salad.

Serves 4

Cold roast duckling meat (see Roast Duckling, page 140)

Salad:

A selection of salad leaves (such as curly endive, oak leaf and crisp Webbs Wonderful lettuce; dandelion; nasturtium), washed and dried

2 bunches watercress, washed and dried

1 orange, peeled, segmented and cut into small pieces

1 bunch spring onions, trimmed and finely sliced on the diagonal, including all the good green parts

Orange Dressing:

Juice of 1 orange, boiled to reduce by half

Dash of wine vinegar

1 teaspoon Dijon mustard

¼ teaspoon clear honey

5 fl oz (150 ml) good-quality olive oil

Strip the ducklings of all good meat remaining on the legs and carcasses. (The carcasses will make excellent stock.) Remove the skin and reserve; cut the meat into attractive strips. Scrape as much fat as possible off the pieces of skin, put them into a saucepan over a low heat and fry gently for a while until the remaining fat runs off. Drain the skin very well on kitchen paper, then cut it into strips and dry-fry for about 30 minutes over a very gentle heat, covering for the last 10 minutes, until golden and crunchy – the strips should not be at all burned so be sure to keep the heat as low as possible.

Meanwhile, prepare and combine all the salad ingredients and arrange them beautifully on 4 plates. Add the strips of duckling meat.

When you are ready to serve, combine the dressing ingredients by shaking them together in a screw-top jar. Gently warm the dressing in a saucepan and pour it over the salad. Garnish with the cracklings. Serve immediately.

Roast goose

Young goose is flavoursome and rich, although the breast meat tends to dryness. An excellent cooking method for it is that given for Roast Duckling (see page 140). This allows a preliminary roasting time to release a good amount of the goose fat. (Goose fat is superbly flavoured and will keep for several weeks in the refrigerator or may be frozen. Use it for sautéing potatoes and other foods – you need far less of it for frying than if you use butter.) With an oven-ready goose, allow 1 lb (450 g) per person, but with a smaller goose allow a larger quantity per person as the ratio of meat to bone is smaller.

Prepare a good stock using the giblets, trimmings and flavouring vegetables as described for Roast Duckling. When you have poured off all the fat from the preliminary roasting at gas mark 7, 425°F (220°C), put the goose, breast side down, in the roasting tin and pour over all the stock. Turn the oven down to gas mark 4, 350°F (180°C), and continue cooking for 2–3 hours for a bird of 9–12 lb (4–5.5 kg). Turn the bird on to its back for the final 30 minutes, but do not baste at this stage. By now the breast meat will have undergone a succulent combination of braising and roasting. Remove the goose from the tin, drain well, put on a warmed platter and leave to rest for 15 minutes – longer won't hurt, but keep it covered. Follow the procedure described for Roast Duckling to make a grease-free well-flavoured gravy.

For goose, I prefer to cook a separate stuffing. As the meat is rich, a fairly plain herbed stuffing is good, or lightly cooked sliced apples and prunes.

Cold left-over goose is delicious, and may be served with salads or in sandwiches.

Goose pie

Here is a very simple but delicious pie recipe which I have adapted from Mary Hooper's Everyday Meals *published in 1883, when I suppose goose was more 'everyday' than now. Well-flavoured left-over game birds would probably work as well as goose in this dish. Serve with Brussels sprouts, glazed turnips or tiny onions and a dish of chestnut stuffing.*

Serves 4–6

Left-over meat from cooked goose and its carcass

1 onion, peeled and chopped

1–2 carrots, peeled and chopped

1–2 sticks celery, sliced

1 bunch herbs (bay leaf, parsley, thyme)

Pinch of salt

10 black peppercorns, crushed

About 1½ pints (900 ml) water or a mixture of water and dry white wine

2 quantities Apple Sauce (see page 109)

6 oz (175 g) shortcrust pastry (see page 72), made with goose fat if possible, or ½ quantity potato pastry (see page 118) or ½ quantity suet pastry (see page 160)

A little milk or beaten egg to glaze

First cut the goose meat into equal-sized pieces, removing the bones and skin, and set aside. Put the bones, skin and crushed carcass into a large heavy saucepan, add the vegetables, herbs and seasoning, cover with water or wine and water and simmer for 1½ hours. Strain, then return to the wiped-out saucepan and boil to reduce until 10 fl oz (300 ml) strong well-flavoured gravy is left. Allow to cool. Then, using a spoon followed by absorbent kitchen paper, skim and blot off all the fat. This can be done in advance.

When you are ready to cook the pie, pre-heat the oven to gas mark 6, 400°F (200°C). Put a thin layer of Apple Sauce in the bottom of a deepish tart dish and lay all the goose meat on top. Over this spread another layer of apple sauce and pour in as much gravy as the pie will hold. (As there is no other seasoning, the gravy will require to be made very tasty with pepper and salt.) Roll out the pastry in the usual way and use it to cover the pie. Brush with a little milk or beaten egg and bake in the oven for 15 minutes. Then turn the oven down to gas mark 4, 350°F (180°C) and bake for a further 25–30 minutes or until golden-brown and cooked through. Serve hot.

Party salad of marbled eggs with young vegetables and fruits in a light spicy dressing

This is an elegant dish which makes a beautiful centrepiece for a summer supper party or special occasion. The combination of ingredients is exotic and the contrasting flavours exquisite. Obviously, if you cannot find the vegetables that I suggest below, think of others to partner the fruits – whatever is sympathetic, seasonal and available.

If you can buy smoked eggs – or you can smoke them yourself in a home smoker – these would be even more interesting than the marbled tea eggs.

In view of the possibility of salmonella contamination of raw eggs, prepare the mayonnaise using cooked egg as described on page 217.

Serves 4–6

4–6 eggs

1 pot of cold tea

1 tablespoon dark soy sauce

2 heads cos lettuce, curly endive or Chinese leaves

About 4 oz (110 g) tender young broad beans, cooked *al dente*

6 artichoke hearts, prepared

About 6 oz (175 g) tender young asparagus, cooked

About 6 oz (175 g) fennel, trimmed and sliced

1 mango, peeled and cut into chunks, or 2 bananas, peeled and sliced on the diagonal

1 grapefruit, peeled, segmented and sliced into small pieces

Whole mint leaves to garnish

Dressing:

5 fl oz (150 ml) Alternative Mayonnaise (see page 215)

5 fl oz (150 ml) fromage frais or natural yoghurt

1 teaspoon mild curry powder

1 tablespoon chopped fresh mint leaves (or to taste)

Hard-boil the eggs for 8 minutes, then cool. Using the back of a teaspoon, gently tap the shells all over until they are totally crazed and cracked but still intact. Now simmer them for 1 hour in the tea and soy sauce. Cool and shell. They should have a beautiful, coffee-coloured, marbled appearance and be subtly impregnated with the tea and soy sauce flavour.

Wash the salad leaves, dry well, cover and set aside in the refrigerator to keep crisp. Combine all the dressing ingredients and set aside.

Prepare the vegetables and fruits with care, collecting the grapefruit and mango juice that escapes and adding it to the dressing. (Mangos are difficult to prepare: try peeling off the skin, then paring off nice slices from around the stone. It is impossible to remove the stone by the 'avocado method'.) Put the prepared vegetables and fruits into a large mixing bowl and pour the dressing all over. Combine very gently with your fingers, taking care not to break up the fruit.

Now assemble the dish. Line a large serving platter with the salad leaves – especially around the border. Make a nest of the marbled eggs in the centre, then spoon the dressed vegetables and fruits around them. Garnish with whole mint leaves. Serve with warm soft bread rolls, warm pasta or tiny new potatoes mixed with some of the reserved dressing.

Game

Grilled young grouse

Most people would agree that the grouse is the aristocrat of game birds. It is also generally agreed that it should not be hung for too long (see page 32) and that simple roasting or grilling (as in this recipe) are the best methods of cooking.

I like grouse with a slightly sweet sauce, and since blackberries are in season with the first grouse I add a smidgin of my home-made jelly and garnish the dish with a few whole blackberries. Brussels sprouts make a good accompaniment.

Serves 4

4 young grouse, plucked and cleaned

1 oz (25 g) butter

2 shallots, peeled and finely chopped

1 carrot, peeled and diced

1 stick celery, finely sliced

½ bottle red wine

1–2 teaspoons good-quality blackberry jelly or preserve

Freshly ground black pepper

2 tablespoons sunflower oil

A few blackberries to garnish (optional)

First rinse the grouse inside and out and pat dry with kitchen paper. Using a pair of kitchen scissors or game shears, cut down the middle of the back of each bird, turn it over and flatten it. Turn it back, cut off the back bones and wings as neatly as possible and remove the wishbone; break up these pieces of carcass. You should now be left with a fairly tidy, flattish breast and legs.

Now make the sauce. Melt the butter in a saucepan, sweat out the shallots, carrot and celery, then add the grouse bones and red wine. Simmer for about 20 minutes, then strain the stock and return it to the pan. Boil hard to reduce it to a third of its original volume – you should have a syrupy concentrated sauce – then add the blackberry jelly to taste and heat through. Keep warm.

Pre-heat the grill and get it good and hot. Season the grouse breasts with pepper and brush each side with a little of the oil. Grill the grouse for 8–10 minutes, turning occasionally and basting with more oil if necessary. To test if the grouse is ready, prick the breast: the juice that runs out should be pink, not clear. Do not overcook the grouse: err on the side of undercooking as the breasts will continue to cook a little when removed from the heat. Serve the grouse garnished with blackberries, and hand the sauce separately.

Roast mallard with cider and orange sauce

The beautiful flavour of mallard is complemented with a light fruity sauce in this very easy recipe. The breasts should be as rare as you like them: do not overcook the duck or it will become tough. Two young hen mallards should serve four people, but if you are feeding large appetites you will need an extra bird. Braised celery or baby leeks are a good accompaniment.

Serves 4

2 mallards, plucked and cleaned

10 fl oz (300 ml) dry cider

2 shallots, peeled and finely chopped

Juice of 2 oranges

2 matchsticks of orange rind

Pinch of salt

Freshly ground black pepper

2 tablespoons whipping cream

Pre-heat the oven to gas mark 7, 425°F (220°C).

Wipe the mallards with dampened kitchen paper, pat dry and put them in a roasting tin. Pour 5 fl oz (150 ml) of the cider over them and roast in the oven for 20–25 minutes.

While this is happening, put the shallots, the remaining 5 fl oz (150 ml) cider, the orange juice and matchsticks of rind into a saucepan and boil hard to reduce to a third of its original volume. Strain. Rinse out the pan and return the liquid to it to keep warm.

Remove the mallards from the oven and let them rest in a warm place for a few minutes. Carve off the breasts and – if they are tender enough – the legs too. Keep warm on a warmed serving plate. Crush or break up the carcasses and return them, together with any juices that have run out of the birds while they were keeping warm, to the roasting tin. Simmer on top of the stove for 15 minutes, then strain into the reduced cider and orange juice. Bring to the boil and reduce to a thickish sauce. Season to taste with salt and pepper. Remove from the heat and stir in the cream.

To serve, slice the mallard breasts and arrange with the legs (if using) on warmed plates. Pour the sauce over.

Braised partridge with pumpkin

Partridge is one of my favourite game birds. When young and tender, its flavour, like that of most young game birds, is simply superb. Five days is about the right hanging time for partridge, otherwise its fine flavour becomes too gamy. (See page 31 for more information on hanging and other aspects of preparing game.) If you are not sure of the age of your partridge, this stewing method is especially splendid: it is also excellent for pheasant and quail. The delicate and faintly earthy flavour of pumpkin is marvellous with game, and it is in the shops for the season. Plain boiled or sautéed potatoes go well with this dish. If you cannot obtain pumpkin, cabbage, parsnips and lentils are also good accompaniments.

Serves 4

2 plump partridges, plucked and cleaned

½ tablespoon sunflower oil

2 rashers bacon, de-rinded and cut into strips

2 tablespoons brandy (optional)

1 glass white wine

5 fl oz (150 ml) home-made veal or chicken stock

1 bay leaf

1 sprig parsley

1½–2 lb (700–900 g) pumpkin

Pinch of salt

Freshly ground black pepper

Pinch of freshly grated nutmeg

1–2 tablespoons cream

½ oz (10 g) chilled butter

Pre-heat the oven to gas mark 4, 350°F (180°C). Rinse the birds inside and out and pat dry with kitchen paper.

In a small, heavy, flameproof casserole heat the oil and gently fry the strips of bacon in it until the fat runs. Turn up the heat, add the partridges and fry them in the hot fat until they are browned on all sides. If you are using brandy, warm this slightly in a small dry saucepan or in a ladle over a gas flame. Light the brandy and pour it flaming over the birds. Shake the pan as the flames subside, then add the wine, stock, bay leaf and parsley. Position the partridges so that they are breast side down and heat until scarcely simmering. Cover the casserole tightly, transfer to the oven and cook for about 40 minutes or until the birds are tender – older birds will need longer. (You could, of course, cook them entirely on top of the stove if you wish.)

Meanwhile, cut the pumpkin into manageable wedges, scrape out the inner fibrous part and the seeds (these can be toasted for use later), peel off the skin and slice the flesh. Simmer the slices of pumpkin in a covered pan in 2 tablespoons water (they will make plenty of water of their own) for about 20 minutes or until very soft. Strain off any excess liquid and purée the pumpkin in a food processor or liquidiser. Return to the pan over the heat to let it dry out somewhat. Season with salt and pepper, add nutmeg and stir in a little cream. Keep warm.

Now, using a slotted spoon, take the partridges from the casserole and put them on a warm plate. Carve off the breasts and legs, set aside and keep warm. Crush the carcasses and return them to the cooking liquid in the casserole. Simmer for a further 5 minutes on top of the stove, then strain into a clean saucepan. Boil the sauce to reduce somewhat and whisk in ½ oz (10 g) chilled butter.

Arrange the breasts and legs with the sauce on 4 warmed plates, together with decorative mounds of pumpkin. Serve immediately.

Pheasant stew

This is a good way of cooking older or slightly damaged game birds (see page 33 for more information on pheasants).

Serves 4–6

2 tablespoons sunflower oil

2 medium onions, peeled and sliced

2 carrots, peeled and cut into chunks

2 parsnips, peeled and cut into chunks

2 sticks celery, sliced

2 pheasants, plucked and cleaned

10 fl oz–1 pint (300–570 ml) white wine

1 bunch herbs (parsley, thyme, bay leaf)

2 matchsticks thinly pared orange rind

2 matchsticks thinly pared lemon rind

Pinch of salt

Freshly ground black pepper

2–3 teaspoons cranberry or redcurrant jelly

Pre-heat the oven to gas mark 1, 275°F (140°C).

In a heavy-bottomed frying-pan heat the oil and brown all the vegetables. Using a slotted spoon transfer these to a deep flameproof casserole dish large enough to take both birds comfortably. Trim any remaining excess fatty bits from the pheasants before giving them a quick wash both inside and out and patting dry with kitchen paper. Brown the birds all over in the frying-pan and put them breast side down into the casserole. Add a cupful of wine to the frying-pan and continue to heat, stirring constantly to loosen all the meat juices that have stuck to the bottom, then pour into the casserole. Add the herbs and orange and lemon rind and season to taste with salt and pepper. Pour in enough wine to cover. Heat very slowly until barely simmering, cover with a tight-fitting lid, then put into the oven and cook for about 2 hours or until the pheasants are absolutely tender.

Using slotted spoons transfer the birds and vegetables to a warm plate. Take all the meat off the pheasants and return the carcasses to the stock in the casserole, together with any juices that meanwhile have seeped from the birds. Simmer for a further 10 minutes. Cool the stock and blot off any fat from the surface with kitchen paper. Now reduce the stock to thicken it a little. Check the seasoning, adjusting if necessary, and stir in the cranberry or redcurrant jelly. Return the meat and vegetables to the casserole, heat through without boiling and keep warm until ready to serve.

Roast pheasant with white wine and grapes

This is a very easy recipe with a nice nutty stuffing and delicious pan juices to serve. See page 33 for information about pheasants.

Serves 4–6

2 pheasants, plucked and cleaned

2 lbs (900 g) seedless grapes

4 oz (110 g) pistachio nuts, chopped

4 oz (110 g) hazel nuts, chopped

A little sunflower oil

1–2 glasses fruity white wine

4–6 rashers green streaky bacon

1 bay leaf

1 sprig rosemary

Pinch of salt

Freshly ground black pepper

1 small nut of butter or 1 tablespoon cream (optional)

Pre-heat the oven to gas mark 5, 375°F (190°C).

Rinse the pheasants inside and out and pat dry with kitchen paper. Wash the grapes, mash half of them roughly with a fork and combine with the nuts, then add half of the remaining whole grapes. Stuff this mixture into the cavities of the birds and truss them (see page 34).

Heat a little oil in a roasting tin and turn the birds in it to brown them. Remove the birds for a moment, then add a little wine to the tin and continue to heat, stirring constantly to loosen all the juices stuck to the bottom. Return the birds to the roasting tin, cover the breasts with bacon, pour in more wine to a depth of 1–1½ inches (2.5–3 cm), add the bay leaf and rosemary and roast in the oven for 15 minutes. Now baste the pheasants with the juices and add most of the remaining whole grapes to the pan, reserving a few for use as a garnish. Roast for a further 40 minutes or until the birds are tender. Remove them and keep warm for 5 minutes before carving.

Meanwhile, using kitchen paper, blot any fat from the surface of the cooking juices and reduce these as necessary by boiling hard to form the sauce. Season to taste with salt and pepper. A nut of butter or 1 tablespoon cream may also be added if you wish. Serve the slices of pheasant and stuffing with the sauce poured over and garnished with the reserved grapes.

Quails in wine with garlic croûtes

A delightfully light and easy dish, full of flavour and quick to cook. (See page 42 for information about quails.) If you are in a hurry, you could leave out the finishing stages of the sauce and just serve the birds with the reduced cooking liquid. Dried porcini (ceps) have a rich assertive flavour compared to fresh button mushrooms and make a distinct contribution to this dish.

Serves 4

8 slices good white bread, crusts removed

4–5 cloves garlic, peeled

8 quails, plucked and cleaned

3 oz (75 g) seasoned flour

3 oz (75 g) unsalted butter

8 juniper berries, crushed

2 oz (50 g) dried whole *porcini* (ceps), soaked (see page 200), and their liquor

15 fl oz (400 ml) red wine

2 shallots, peeled and finely chopped

Dash of red wine vinegar

2 tablespoons dry vermouth

Pinch of salt

Freshly ground black pepper

First lay the slices of bread on a baking sheet and bake in the oven at gas mark 2, 300°F (150°C) until they are crisp and dry. Allow to cool, then rub each side with a garlic clove until all the garlic has worn away. Set aside.

Rinse the quails inside and out and pat dry with kitchen paper. Roll them in the seasoned flour to coat lightly. Heat 1 oz (25 g) of the butter in a large heavy frying-pan and brown the birds all over. Add the juniper berries, the *porcini* (and their soaking liquid) or mushrooms and the red wine and heat until just under simmering point. Adjust the heat, cover the pan and cook the quails very gently at just under simmering for about 25 minutes or until they are tender. Using a large slotted spoon lift the quails and *porcini* out of the pan, transfer them to a warmed dish and keep warm. Strain the cooking liquid and keep warm.

Now make the sauce. Melt another 1 oz (25 g) of the butter in a saucepan and cook the shallots in this very gently until they are soft but not brown.

Add a dash of vinegar and the vermouth and cook until the liquid has almost vanished. Now add the strained cooking liquid and boil hard until reduced by half. Strain again, re-heat, season to taste with salt and pepper, and finish by whisking in the remaining 1 oz (25 g) butter.

Serve the quails on the garlic croûtes with the sauce poured over and garnished with the *porcini*.

Game terrine

Though not strictly speaking a main course, a home-made terrine of this kind makes a fine meal served with your own cranberry sauce, a green salad and lots of crusty bread. Apart from its delicious simplicity, all the cooking is done at least a day in advance – and then the whole meal can be on the table in a trice. This is also a sensible way to use old or damaged birds (see also Game Pudding, page 160).

Serves 6

2 old grouse, pigeons or mallards or 1 pheasant, plucked and cleaned

3 tablespoons brandy

3 tablespoons Madeira

A little grated orange rind

1–2 tablespoons sunflower oil

1 onion, peeled and finely chopped

1 carrot, peeled and diced

1 stick celery, sliced

1 bay leaf

1 glass red wine

Freshly ground black pepper

2 lb (900 g) belly pork (about two thirds lean to one third fat), minced or chopped in a food processor

2 cloves garlic, peeled and chopped

Good pinch of ground allspice

Good pinch of ground cloves

Pinch of salt

Bay leaves and juniper berries to garnish

Rinse the birds inside and out and pat dry with kitchen paper. To remove the breasts and leg meat from the carcasses, it is easier to stiffen the birds by cooking them slightly first. So pre-heat the oven to gas mark 6, 400°F (200°C), and cook the birds in it (without any fat or liquid) for about 4–5 minutes. Now remove the breast sections and take the meat from the legs, discarding the skin. Cut the breasts into chunky strips and place them in a glass or earthenware dish with the leg meat. Pour over the brandy and Madeira, add the grated orange rind and leave to marinate for at least 1 hour, turning occasionally.

Heat the oil in a large pan, add half the chopped onion, the carrot and celery and the broken up carcasses of the birds and brown. Then add the bay leaf, wine, pepper and water to cover and simmer for 1 hour. Strain and then boil hard to reduce to about 6 tablespoons.

Now fork the remaining onion into the minced belly pork, together with the chopped leg meat from the marinade, the garlic, spices, and some salt and pepper. Add the 6 tablespoons reduced stock and beat well until all is evenly blended. To check the seasoning, fry a little ball of this mixture, taste, and adjust the spices and seasoning accordingly.

Pre-heat the oven to gas mark 3, 325°F (170°C). To assemble the terrine, put half the pork mixture into a terrine or loaf tin. (It should not be necessary to grease the container if it is well used, because the fat in the pork should prevent any sticking.) Make a layer of the breast meat, trickling over the brandy and Madeira marinade, and cover with the remaining pork mixture. Decorate the top with juniper berries and bay leaves. Cover with a lid or double thickness of aluminium foil. Put the terrine into a roasting tin and pour enough boiling water into the tin to come about half-way up the sides of the terrine. Cook in the oven for 1¼ hours. Remove from the oven and allow to cool. Take off the lid if you were using one, cover with aluminium foil and place a weight on top of the terrine – a bag of rice or a heavy object resting on a chopping board will do. Chill in the refrigerator until set – preferably overnight. There will be a beautifully flavoured jelly around this terrine when you turn it out to slice before serving.

Wild rabbit braised with lemon, anchovies and herbs

The rabbits that scatter across the gorse-covered downs when I go for a dawn jog are much leaner and fitter than I'll ever be! However, though they are very tasty, they do tend to be stringy. Long slow cooking is the answer, for which you will need a heavy flameproof casserole. You can, of course, use frozen or farmed rabbit (see page 43 for information on choosing rabbit) if you cannot obtain the wild variety. Serve the dish with grilled tomatoes, crusty bread and a crisp green salad, or with lentils, butter beans or chickpeas.

Serves 4

1 rabbit, skinned and jointed, or 1½–2 lb (700–900 g) rabbit pieces

4–5 tablespoons good-quality olive oil

3–4 tablespoons lemon juice

Freshly ground black pepper

2 large onions, peeled and thickly sliced

8 tinned anchovy fillets, pounded to a rough paste

1 tablespoon chopped fresh green herbs

4 ripe tomatoes

1–2 fat cloves garlic, peeled and finely chopped

Pre-heat the oven to gas mark 4, 350°F (180°C).

Wash the pieces of rabbit, pat dry with kitchen paper and put them into a heavy flameproof casserole with 3–4 tablespoons of the olive oil, the lemon juice, a scant 10 fl oz (300 ml) water, some pepper, the onions, anchovies and herbs. Heat on top of the stove until barely simmering and let the casserole get good and hot as you shake it and give a little stir to blend all the ingredients for the cooking liquid. Now cover the casserole tightly, put it into the oven and cook for 1½–2 hours (the dish won't spoil by long cooking). When the rabbit is tender, you can keep it warm until you are ready to eat.

Pre-heat the grill and spread a sheet of lightly oiled aluminium foil on the grill rack. Skin the tomatoes, slice them thickly, scatter with the chopped garlic and some pepper, and drizzle over a little olive oil. Place them on the prepared rack and grill for about 5 minutes or until sizzling.

Serve the rabbit garnished with the grilled tomatoes.

Game pudding

This is another very good recipe for cooking game birds (grouse, partridge, wild duck, pigeon and so on) that you know to be old or whose age you are uncertain of. I have adapted it from Margaret Costa's Four Seasons Cookery Book. *Because game in pies tends to dryness, beef is added here, along with a well-flavoured gravy. Beef also has the effect of evening out the taste for those who do not care for an overpowering gamy flavour. Serve with fresh seasonal vegetables, plus extra gravy made with the unused game stock.*

Serves 4

2–3 game birds (depending on size)

1–1¼ lb (450–550 g) rump or lean chuck steak

Seasoned flour

8 oz (225 g) mushrooms, wiped

1 oz (25 g) butter

1 small onion, peeled and grated or very finely chopped

Marinade:

1 glass red wine

2 tablespoons olive oil

6 juniper berries, crushed

Freshly ground black pepper

Stock:

1 onion, peeled and chopped

1 carrot, peeled and chopped

1 stick celery, sliced

1 bunch herbs (bay leaf, parsley)

Pinch of salt

Freshly ground black pepper

A little port or redcurrant jelly (optional)

Suet Pastry:

12 oz (350 g) self-raising flour

Good pinch of salt

6 oz (175 g) shredded suet

Bee's knees (page 177), Garlicky beefburgers with soured cream (page 75), and Grilled pork with sweet and sour plum sauce (page 112)

If possible, start the preparation the day before you intended serving the pudding. Rinse the birds inside and out and pat dry with kitchen paper. Remove the breast meat from the birds, discarding the skin, and cut the meat into neat pieces. Combine the marinade ingredients, pour over the meat in a glass or earthenware bowl and set aside in a cool place for several hours or overnight. Break up the carcasses of the birds and put them with the legs into a large saucepan. Add all the other stock ingredients, cover with cold water, bring to the boil and simmer for 2 hours. Strain, boil fiercely to reduce somewhat and concentrate the flavour, and add a little port or redcurrant jelly if you wish. Cool and refrigerate.

When you are ready to cook, trim the steak, cut it into bite-sized pieces and dust with seasoned flour. Fry the mushrooms (whole if small, sliced if large) very gently in a little butter to seal.

To prepare the pastry, sift together the flour and salt and mix in the suet. Add enough cold water to form an elastic dough. Lightly but thoroughly butter a 2 pint (1.1 litre) pudding basin. Roll out two thirds of the pastry on a floured board and use it to line the pudding basin, taking care not to stretch the pastry. Lift the breasts from the marinade and fill the pudding, beginning with a layer of steak followed by a layer of marinaded breasts, then a few mushrooms and a little onion. Continue in this way until you almost reach the top. Pour in enough stock to come three quarters of the way up the basin. Roll out the remaining pastry to form a lid and cover the pudding with it, damping the edges with a little water and pressing well to seal. Cover first with a sheet of buttered greaseproof paper, then with either a pudding cloth or a double thickness of aluminium foil. Stand the basin in a large saucepan of boiling water and steam for 3–4 hours. You may find that you need to add more boiling water to the pan occasionally – but it *must* be boiling, as adding cold water will arrest the cooking process.

Glazed gammon with Cumberland sauce (page 115), Party salad of marbled eggs with young vegetables and fruits in a light spicy dressing (page 146), and Chicory, leek and sage flan (page 194)

Two simple dishes from one rabbit

The following two dishes can be produced from one young, preferably wild rabbit. In the first, the saddle is simply marinated in the same ingredients given for Saddle of Hare (page 167), and the second is a versatile casserole using the remaining pieces of rabbit.

Saddle of rabbit with mushroom pâté

Serve with plain boiled rice and grilled spring onions or baby leeks.

Serves 2

1 saddle of young rabbit

1 quantity Marinade (see page 167)

1–2 tablespoons sunflower oil or 1–2 oz (25–50 g) butter

2–3 tablespoons Mushroom Pâté (see page 62)

Remove the meat lengthways from the saddle and cut into small neat pieces. Cover with the marinade in a glass or earthenware bowl and leave in a cool place for several hours, turning occasionally.

When you are ready to cook, drain the rabbit and pat dry. Heat the oil or butter very gently in a frying-pan and slowly fry the pieces of rabbit in it until brown, cooked through and tender. Warm the Mushroom Pâté gently in a saucepan.

To serve, divide the rabbit pieces between 2 warmed plates and spoon the pâté alongside.

Rabbit in cider with prunes

Serves 2–3

4 rabbit joints

1 tablespoon seasoned flour

8 oz (225 g) streaky bacon or *pancetta* (cured spiced belly of pork)

1–2 tablespoons sunflower or peanut (groundnut) oil

2 large onions, peeled, halved and thinly sliced to form crescents

1 clove garlic, peeled and chopped

10 fl oz (300 ml) cider or dry white or red wine

10 fl oz (300 ml) stock

1 bunch herbs (bay leaf, parsley, thyme)

Pinch of salt

Freshly ground black pepper

4 oz (110 g) stoned prunes

Croûtons and chopped parsley to garnish

First wash the rabbit joints and pat dry with kitchen paper. Dust in seasoned flour and wrap each piece in a strip of bacon or *pancetta*, securing with wooden cocktail sticks.

Heat the oil in a heavy frying-pan and gently brown the onions in it. Towards the end of their cooking time add the garlic. Transfer them to a flameproof casserole and set aside. Then brown the rabbit pieces all over in the frying-pan and add these to the casserole too. Pour the cider or wine and stock over the rabbit, add the herbs, salt and pepper and gently heat until barely simmering. Cover and continue simmering very gently for 1–1½ hours or until the rabbit is tender. Fifteen minutes before the end of the cooking time, add the prunes.

To serve, arrange the rabbit pieces on an attractive shallow platter and keep warm while you quickly boil the sauce to reduce and thicken it somewhat. Pour it all over the rabbit and strew with croûtons and lots of chopped parsley.

Mustard rabbit

There are many recipes for this classic dish, but here is a good foolproof one. My sister cooked it for us, and we all remarked on the clean taste and texture of the rabbit with a sauce that had a subtle tang rather than an overwhelming blast of mustard flavour. Serve with mashed potatoes and peas.

Serves 4

1 young rabbit, skinned and jointed

Pinch of salt

A little vinegar (optional)

4 tablespoons English or continental mustard

2 tablespoons olive oil

1 onion, peeled and sliced

1–2 fat cloves garlic, peeled and finely chopped

2–3 oz (50–75 g) smoked bacon, diced

Seasoned flour for coating

Freshly ground black pepper

10 fl oz (300 ml) single cream

Begin the day before you intend serving the dish if possible. First soak the rabbit joints in lightly salted water, or water acidulated with a little vinegar, for 1–2 hours. Drain and pat dry. Smother with the mustard and leave, covered, in a cool place for a few hours or overnight.

When you are ready to cook, heat the olive oil in a large flameproof casserole and gently fry the onion in it for a few minutes until soft but not brown, adding the chopped garlic for the final minute. Using a slotted spoon, transfer to a plate and set aside. Now gently fry the bacon until the fat runs and transfer this to the plate. Dust the rabbit joints in the seasoned flour and brown them all over in the casserole. Return the onion, garlic and bacon to the casserole, season with salt and pepper and cook very gently on top of the stove for about 30 minutes. Then stir in the cream and continue cooking at barely simmering point for a further 30–45 minutes or until the rabbit is tender.

Jugged hare

'What exactly is *jugged hare?*' people always ask, intrigued by the notion of jugs and furry animals. It is in fact a slow-cooked stew: when cooked authentically, the skinned and jointed hare is placed in a jug or crock with liquid and other ingredients, then stood in a deep pan of hot water and cooked slowly in a low oven. Nowadays this is more usually done in an everyday flameproof casserole, tightly sealed. To the joy of the cook, the additional ingredients are flexible; and the wonderful rich cooking aroma will have your waiting guests or family sitting in quiet corners of the home and swooning in anticipation of their supper. Ask your game dealer for advice about the age of the hare and if or how long it has been hung (see page 43). If you care to, use the blood for the final stages of the gravy – some game butchers sell this separately. Keep the saddle for the recipe on page 167. Forcemeat balls and redcurrant jelly are traditionally served with Jugged Hare.

Serves 4–6

1 hare, skinned and jointed, liver and blood reserved

2–3 tablespoons olive oil

4 rashers streaky bacon, de-rinded and cut into 1 inch (2.5 cm) squares

1–2 medium onions, peeled and quartered

1 pint (570 ml) good stock

Red wine (optional)

Pinch of salt

1 bunch herbs (bay leaf, parsley, thyme)

6 black peppercorns

6 allspice berries

6 cloves

1 carrot, peeled and cut into chunks

2 sticks celery, sliced

Juice of 1 lemon and 1 piece of rind

20 button onions, peeled

Beurre manié (see page 16)

1 glass port

Pre-heat the oven to gas mark 1, 275°F (140°C). Do not wash the hare pieces – the blood contributes to the characteristic gamy flavour.

Heat a little of the olive oil in a heavy-bottomed frying-pan, add the bacon and fry gently until the fat runs. Transfer to a plate. Gently fry the onions until soft and slightly coloured and transfer these also to the plate. Now add the remaining oil to the pan, put in the joints of hare and brown them all over – you may have to do this in several batches. Pack the joints into a lidded flameproof casserole and add the bacon and onion. Heat the stock in the frying-pan, scraping up any juices stuck to the bottom, and pour into the casserole. Add red wine and/or water to cover well. Season with salt, push in the herbs, peppercorns, allspice, cloves, carrot, celery, lemon juice and rind and heat on top of the stove until just simmering. Cover with a double thickness of aluminium foil and the lid, crimping the foil well around the rim to seal completely. Cook in the oven for 3 hours. Boil the button onions in water for 10 minutes or until tender and set aside.

Transfer the hare (which will by now be very tender, so take care that the joints do not fall apart) to a warmed ovenproof serving dish, cover and keep warm. Strain the cooking liquid into a saucepan, pressing well on the vegetables to extract all the juices. Bring the liquid to simmering point and stir in knobs of *beurre manié* to thicken the sauce. Add the port. At this stage add the mashed liver of the hare if you wish and cook for a further 10 minutes. Remove the sauce from the heat and allow to cool very slightly. Add the blood now to thicken the sauce further if you like. To do this, spoon a little of the warm sauce into the blood and mix well, then tip the mixture into the pan of sauce and re-heat gently: on no account must it be allowed to boil or it will curdle.

To serve, re-heat the button onions and garnish the platter of hare with them. Pour over some of the sauce.

Saddle of hare

For this roast, young hare (leveret) is best. You could ask your game butcher to help by chining out the saddle and releasing the fillets to make carving easier. Serve with wild rice and steamed haricots verts.

Serves 4

1 saddle of hare
½ tablespoon olive oil

Marinade:

2 glasses red wine

1 sprig rosemary, bruised

6 juniper berries, crushed

Freshly ground black pepper

Sauce:

1 oz (25 g) unsalted butter

1 shallot, peeled and finely chopped

4–5 tablespoons game stock (see page 160) or good meat stock

1 tablespoon single or whipping cream

Several hours before you are ready to cook, trim the saddle but do not wash it. Mix the marinade ingredients together, combine with the hare in a glass or earthenware bowl, cover and set aside in a cool place for a few hours – older hare should be marinated overnight.

When you are ready to cook, pre-heat the oven to gas mark 8, 450°F (230°C). Lift the saddle from the marinade (reserve the marinade) and pat dry with kitchen paper. Heat the oil in a heavy-bottomed frying-pan and briskly sear the saddle in it to seal, then transfer to a small roasting tin and cook in the oven for 15 minutes. Remove from the oven and keep warm.

Meanwhile, make the sauce. Melt the butter in a small saucepan and gently fry the shallot for a few minutes until soft but not brown. Strain the reserved marinade, add it to the shallot and boil until reduced to a syrupy glaze. Add the stock, reduce by half, draw off the heat and whisk in the cream. Keep warm. Now slice the hare into thin diagonal slices and arrange on 4 warmed dinner plates. Strain a little of the pale rose-coloured sauce over and hand the remaining sauce separately.

A simple venison stew

The meat of young venison is tender and needs only about an hour's cooking. Here is a simple way of preparing it; the recipe following this one is more elaborate and special.

Serve with boiled potatoes or noodles and grilled field mushrooms. The flavour of this stew will be even better if you let it stand in the refrigerator for a day or so before eating it. Be sure to re-heat it gently but thoroughly.

Serves 4

1½ lb (700 g) shoulder of venison

1–2 tablespoons olive oil

2 large onions, peeled and sliced

2 large carrots, peeled and sliced

About 1 pint (570 ml) game stock (see page 160)

Pinch of salt

Freshly ground black pepper

Beurre manié (see page 16; optional)

1–2 tablespoons whipping cream (optional)

Marinade:

2 fat cloves garlic, peeled and chopped

2 glasses red wine

3 tablespoons olive oil

Freshly ground black pepper

If possible, begin making this dish the day before you intend serving it. Trim the venison and cut it into cubes. Combine the marinade ingredients in a glass or earthenware bowl and toss the venison in the marinade. Cover and leave for several hours – preferably overnight.

When you are ready to cook, pre-heat the oven to gas mark 4, 350°F (180°C).

Drain the venison, reserving the marinade, and pat dry. Heat the oil in a heavy flameproof casserole, add the meat and brown it all over. Remove and drain on kitchen paper, then gently fry the onions and carrots until they are softened but not brown. Return the meat to the casserole and add the stock. Skim the oil from the marinade and discard it, then add the remaining marinade to the stew and stir it in. Depending on how well seasoned your stock is, add a little salt and freshly ground black pepper. Cover tightly and cook in the oven for 1–1½ hours or until the venison is tender. The stew should now be of a nice reduced consistency. If you wish, it can be thickened with a knob of *buerre manié*. A little whipping cream may also be stirred in just before serving.

Venison stew with hare

This is an especially delicious combination of meats and the flavour of their stocks. As with cassoulet and other 'major' casseroles, the advance preparation and careful cooking ensures a stunning dish to serve to guests, with the minimum of work for the cook just prior to serving.

If you have used the saddle only from a hare, jug the rest of it (see page 165). Remove all the tender meat from the bones and cut it into neat pieces. At this stage you can put the meat in a basin, cover it with hare stock and vegetables, cool, cover and keep in the refrigerator for up to 3 days.

Make the Simple Venison Stew described on page 168, reducing the marinating time if you are in a hurry. Add all the jugged hare to the stew and re-heat very gently, adding a little more good meat stock if you have it. It will not need thickening. Transfer to a warmed serving dish or tureen and garnish with croûtes.

Grilled venison fillet steaks

These richly flavoured, tender, rare steaks are served with the simplest of sauces. They are superb with celeriac, leeks and sautéed potatoes.

Serves 4

4 venison fillet steaks

Pinch of salt

Freshly ground black pepper

A little oil

2 tablespoons port

8 oz (225 g) redcurrant jelly

1 small stick cinnamon, bruised

3–4 strips thinly pared lemon rind

A few redcurrants to garnish (optional)

Wipe the steaks with dampened kitchen paper and pat dry. Season them with salt and pepper, rub with oil and set aside for 30 minutes.

In a heavy-bottomed saucepan simmer the remaining ingredients for 5 minutes, then remove the cinnamon stick and lemon rind and keep the sauce warm.

When you are ready to cook, pre-heat the grill and oil the grill rack. Grill the steaks for 3–5 minutes on each side, depending on how rare you like them. Pour a little sauce on each of 4 warmed plates, garnish with a few redcurrants if you happen to have them and serve immediately. Hand the remaining sauce separately.

A raised game pie

For a special cold main course, I would certainly recommend this pie – it makes a handsome centrepiece and is much easier to prepare than you might imagine. If you do not have a tin mould for raised pies, you can use a cake tin with a removable bottom.

This recipe should be regarded as a flexible guideline: adapt the filling according to the ingredients available. For instance, two meats – hare and venison or rabbit and venison – may be used, or venison alone. Game pies are often dry, but the pork forcemeat used here solves this problem. If possible, use the liver from hare or other game for the forcemeat.

The pie may be served with Cumberland Sauce (see page 115), or cranberry jelly; it looks splendid presented on a platter surrounded with watercress.

Serves 6–8

2 lb (900 g) game meat (such as hare and lean venison)

Game stock made with bones, trimmings (see page 160) and a split pig's trotter or hock knuckle

6 rashers bacon

Beaten egg to glaze

Marinade:

2 glasses red wine

1 glass olive oil

10 juniper berries, lightly crushed

Pinch of salt

Freshly ground black pepper

Pinch each of grated nutmeg, ground ginger and ground cloves

Forcemeat:

8 oz (225 g) liver (preferably game)

12 oz (350 g) minced lean pork or good-quality sausagemeat

1 fat clove garlic, peeled and chopped

Pinch of salt

Freshly ground black pepper

Pastry:

1 lb (450 g) plain flour

6 oz (175 g) lard

Begin the day before you intend serving the pie if possible. Cut the game into neat pieces or strips. Combine the marinade ingredients, mix with the game in a glass or earthenware bowl and leave in a cool place for several hours or overnight.

Prepare the forcemeat by mincing the liver and combining with the other ingredients: this can be done in a food processor or mincer. Alternatively, chop by hand. A rough chunky texture is best.

Make the game stock in the usual way (see page 160), adding the pig's trotter or hock knuckle so that it will later become gelatinous. Allow to cool and refrigerate until needed. When you are ready to cook, pre-heat the oven to gas mark 6, 400°F (200°C). Assemble the ingredients and have ready a mould or loose-bottomed cake tin.

Now prepare the pastry. Sift the flour into a bowl. Bring the lard and 7 fl oz (200 ml) water to boiling point in a saucepan and pour immediately into the bowl of flour. Mix quickly to form a rather disagreeable-looking paste. To line the mould, you must work quickly or the lard will begin to set and the paste will become brittle. Take two thirds of the paste (keep the remaining third in a warm place), put it into the bottom of the mould and use your fingers to spread it out and bring it up the side, pushing, patting and teasing as you go. It may slip down the side at first, but carry on shaping for it will behave better as it cools.

Next cover the base and part of the side of the pie with the bacon rashers. Put a layer of forcemeat about 1 inch (2.5 cm) thick in the bottom of the lined pastry case, then add a layer of the drained game meat, then more forcemeat and so on until the pie is full.

Roll out the remaining paste to make a lid and cover the pie with it. Trim and seal with a little beaten egg or water. Use the scraps of left-over paste to make leaf or flower shapes and decorate the lid, then brush this with beaten egg. Make a hole in the centre of the pastry lid and insert a small roll of greaseproof paper or aluminium foil to keep the hole open. Bake in the oven for 10 minutes. Turn the heat down to gas mark 2, 300°F (150°C), and continue baking for at least 2–2½ hours. If, after 1 hour, the crust looks as though it is hardening and browning too quickly, cover it loosely with dampened greaseproof paper or aluminium foil.

Take the pie from the oven and leave to cool. Remove the paper or foil roll from the hole in the lid. Warm the stock and carefully pour it into the pie through the hole. Let the pie become cold before removing the tin or mould to serve: it is quite difficult to slice neatly but the joy is in the eating.

Fish
and
Shellfish

Monkfish satay with marinated pears

This dish was cooked for us on the BBC television series 'The Fish Course' by Denis Curtis at one of his glamorous dinner parties. Part of an exotic menu and intended to demonstrate that a main-course fish dish need not be too expensive, it was a huge success. This is my slightly simplified version. Poach the pears the day before and serve the dish with Jersey Royal new potatoes and mange-tout.

Serves 4

3 pears

½ bottle red wine

½ stick cinnamon

1 lb (450 g) monkfish

Marinade:

2 tablespoons light soy sauce

2 cloves garlic, peeled and chopped

2 tablespoons sunflower or peanut (groundnut) oil

1 tablespoon clear honey

1 tablespoon lemon juice

½ teaspoon ground ginger

Pinch of salt

Sauce:

2 oz (50 g) caster sugar

2 tablespoons wine vinegar

Juice of 1 lemon

Juice of 1 orange

15 fl oz (400 ml) light chicken or fish stock

Pinch of salt

Freshly ground pepper

1 oz (25 g) chilled butter

The day before, prepare the pears. Peel, halve and core them and place them in a saucepan in which they fit tightly in a single layer. Cover with the wine and broken cinnamon stick, heat until barely simmering and poach gently until tender. Cool, then put the pears with their liquid in the refrigerator overnight.

Wash the monkfish and pat dry with kitchen paper. Trim it and cut into ¾ inch (2 cm) cubes. In a glass or earthenware dish, whisk together the marinade ingredients, add the monkfish, stir to coat well and leave in a cool place for 4 hours, turning occasionally.

When you are ready to cook, pre-heat the oven to gas mark 4, 350°F (180°C).

To make the sauce, put the sugar and vinegar into a small saucepan and bubble it fiercely over a high heat. Just as the liquid begins to caramelise, add the lemon juice and stir vigorously, then add the orange juice and stock. Simmer until the sauce is reduced to a quarter of its original volume and is thick and syrupy. Season to taste with a little salt and pepper. Remove from the heat and stir in ½ oz (10 g) of the butter, cut into cubes – add the cubes one at a time – to finish the sauce. Keep warm.

Now thread the pieces of monkfish on to 6 skewers, place them on a rack or trivet over a baking dish and cook in the oven for 10 minutes, basting occasionally.

Meanwhile, melt the remaining ½ oz (10 g) butter in a saucepan. Drain the pears, reserving their liquid, add them to the pan and very gently re-heat them. Pour 2–3 tablespoons of the pears' liquid into the pan and baste the fruit continuously until the liquid has almost vanished and the pears are glossy.

To serve, arrange the golden skewers of monkfish on a warmed shallow serving platter and intersperse with the pears. Hand the sauce separately.

Red mullet baked in paper parcels

A simple method for cooking this superb little fish. Remember to cook the mullets with their livers intact – these infuse the fish with their flavour, which is why the French call them the woodcock of the sea.

Serves 4

4 medium red mullet

Pinch of salt

1 oz (25 g) butter

4 tablespoons dry white wine

A little lemon juice

1–2 tablespoons dry sherry

2 tinned anchovy fillets, pounded to a paste, or a dash of anchovy essence

First scale and gut the fish, leaving in the liver. Wash it and pat dry with kitchen paper.

Pre-heat the oven to gas mark 6, 400°F (200°C). Sprinkle a little salt in the belly cavity of the fish. Very lightly butter 4 sheets of greaseproof paper or parchment. Place a fish on each and sprinkle over 1 tablespoon wine and a squeeze of lemon juice per fish. Parcel up the fish by rolling in the paper and twisting each end like a sweet wrapper. Put the parcels on a baking sheet and bake in the oven for up to 20 minutes depending on size – do not overcook.

Now open one end of each parcel and pour all the cooking juices into a small saucepan. Tasting as you go, add a little sherry, boil hard, then stir in a little anchovy paste or essence to taste and finish with a tiny knob of butter. Serve the fish hot in their opened paper parcels with a little sauce poured over.

Bee's knees

During the making of television cookery programmes, the cutting-room floor must be covered with countless clips of food disappearing as gannet camera crews' hands shoot like lightning into the final shots to nab it! Once, when I was involved in shooting a barbecue sequence, John, our sound man, created this recipe, which we filmed and ate: he used giant prawns, but it is equally successful with Dublin Bay prawns (scampi) or white fish such as monkfish or cod.

Serves 3–4

8–10 oz (225–275 g) cod or monkfish fillets, skinned, or 8 giant prawns, shelled

Pinch of salt

Freshly ground black pepper

Juice of ½ lemon

A little oil

4 oz (110 g) smoked salmon, cut into strips

8–10 rashers streaky bacon, de-rinded

Lemon wedges to serve

If you are using fish fillets, check that they are free of all bones, wash them, pat dry with kitchen paper and cut into 1 × 2 inch (2.5 × 5 cm) cubes. Season the fish or prawns (if using) with salt and pepper, put into a glass or earthenware dish, sprinkle with lemon juice and set aside for 30 minutes.

Light the barbecue and get it good and hot, or pre-heat the grill; oil the rack.

When you are ready to cook, roll each piece of fish or each prawn in a strip or two of smoked salmon followed by a rasher of bacon. Thread on to skewers and cook over the barbecue or under the grill for about 8 minutes, turning them as they sizzle. Serve immediately with wedges of lemon – they're the bee's knees!

Swordfish kebabs

The flesh of swordfish is firm and meaty. It is wonderful when simply pan-fried or grilled, and because of its firm texture it makes excellent kebabs for the barbecue.

Serves 4

1–1½ lb (450–700 g) thick swordfish steaks, trimmed and cut into 1 inch (2.5 cm) cubes

Herbed or spiced rice and chopped fresh coriander leaves to serve

Marinade:

4 tablespoons olive oil

4 tablespoons lemon juice

2 fat cloves garlic, crushed, peeled and finely chopped

1 bunch spring onions, trimmed and finely chopped, including all the good green parts

1 inch (2.5 cm) cube fresh root ginger, peeled and grated

1–2 fresh green or red chillies, de-seeded and finely chopped

Pinch of salt

Freshly ground black pepper

Combine the marinade ingredients and cubes of swordfish in an earthenware or glass bowl, cover and leave in a cool place for 4–6 hours. (Do not leave any longer because the texture of the fish will alter as the lemon juice 'cooks' it.)

Pre-heat the grill or light the barbecue and get it good and hot. Lightly oil 4–6 kebab skewers. Load the cubes of fish on to the skewers and grill for 4–6 minutes, turning occasionally and brushing well with the marinade. Arrange on a warmed platter of the rice, drizzle with a little of the remaining marinade, scatter with the chopped coriander and serve straight away.

Baked parrot fish

Spectacular in appearance, parrot fish comes from the Seychelles and may now be seen on many fishmongers' slabs and wet fish counters in good supermarkets in this country. It has a mild fishy flavour and firm flesh.

Serves 2–3

1 large or 2 small parrot fish

2 sticks celery, thinly sliced

4 spring onions, trimmed and thinly sliced, including all the good green parts

1 inch (2.5 cm) cube fresh root ginger, peeled and grated or finely chopped

1 tablespoon sunflower oil

Pinch of salt

Freshly ground black pepper

Juice of 1 lemon or lime

Lemon or lime wedges to serve

Pre-heat the oven to gas mark 6, 400°F (200°C).

Gut and scale the fish, wash the cavity and pat dry inside and out with kitchen paper. Gently fry the celery, spring onions and ginger in a little oil until slightly softened.

Lightly season the fish inside and outside with salt and pepper and sprinkle the cavity with a little lemon or lime juice. Lay the fish on a large sheet of lightly oiled aluminium foil. Stuff with most of the celery, onion and ginger, scattering the remainder over the top of the fish and sprinkling with more lemon or lime juice. Bring up the sides of the foil and crimp to make a loose parcel. Place on a baking sheet and bake in the oven for 25–30 minutes or until the fish is just cooked. Serve with wedges of lemon or lime.

A seafood gratin with breadcrumb crust

This is a versatile recipe using a mild creamy curry-flavoured sauce. Use the freshest white fish of your choice – whatever is in season at the fishmonger's. Serve with new potatoes and peas.

Serves 4

1 lb (450 g) white fish fillets (such as cod, whiting, John Dory, haddock, coley, etc.)

8 oz (225 g) prawns or white crabmeat

Pinch of salt

Freshly ground black pepper

1 glass dry white wine

Squeeze of lemon juice

1 quantity Béchamel Sauce (see page 217)

2 teaspoons curry powder

6 oz (175 g) breadcrumbs

1 oz (25 g) butter

First wash the fish fillets, pat them dry with kitchen paper and cut them into neat pieces. Shell the prawns if necessary and set aside.

Pre-heat the oven to gas mark 6, 400°F (200°C). Lay the pieces of fish in a shallow baking dish, season lightly with salt and pepper and sprinkle over the wine and a squeeze of lemon juice. Cover with a couple of sheets of buttered greaseproof paper and cook in the oven for 5–10 minutes, depending on the thickness of the fish pieces. Do not overcook.

Meanwhile, make the béchamel sauce in the usual way, adding the curry powder as you are cooking out the flour and butter. Pour all the cooking liquor from the baked fish into the sauce, stir well in and cook for a few more minutes, tasting as you go and adjusting the seasoning as necessary to achieve a smooth, creamy, mild-flavoured sauce. Arrange the fish and prawns or crabmeat in a gratin dish and cover with the sauce. Sprinkle with the breadcrumbs and a few small scraps of butter. Pop back into the oven for a few minutes to brown the top or brown under the grill before serving.

Halibut à la QE2

Carl Winkler, jovial chef de cuisine on the QE2, *demonstrated this dish to me down below in the vast gleaming galley when we were filming the BBC television series 'The Fish Course'. Parcelling the fish with wine and a* julienne *of vegetables is a good method for halibut, which has superb firm white flesh but tends to dryness. Carl dished it on a bed of spinach, trickled over a little saffron-flavoured sauce and added tiny new potatoes and a herb garnish. I have adapted this slightly for the home kitchen.*

Serves 4

4 halibut steaks

A little oil

Pinch of salt

Freshly ground white pepper

4 oz (110 g) white part of leek, cut into *julienne* strips

4 oz (110 g) carrot, peeled and cut into *julienne* strips

4 oz (110 g) chilled unsalted butter

8 tablespoons Noilly Prat

2 lb (900 g) spinach, well washed and trimmed

Pinch of saffron threads

Tiny boiled new potatoes to serve

Pre-heat the oven to gas mark 7, 425°F (220°C).
    Wash the fish steaks and pat them dry. Cut out 4 pieces of aluminium foil large enough to wrap each steak generously. Brush the foil very lightly with oil.
    Place a steak in the centre of each sheet of foil. Season lightly with salt and pepper and arrange a little of the leek and carrot *juliennes* neatly along each steak so that it is pleasing to the eye. Cut 2 oz (50 g) of the butter into small pieces and dot the steaks with these. Bring up the edges of each foil sheet and, before crimping it into a loose but airtight parcel, splash 2 tablespoons Noilly Prat into each one. Place the closed parcels on a baking sheet and cook in the hottest part of the oven for 15 minutes.
    Meanwhile, cook the spinach in the usual way, chop coarsely and season lightly with salt and pepper. Melt ½ oz (10 g) of the butter and stir it into the spinach. Keep warm.
    Take the fish from the oven. Open the end of each parcel and carefully tip the cooking juices into a small saucepan. Re-seal the parcels and keep in a

warm place while you make the sauce. Add the saffron to the pan and very gently re-heat the fish cooking juices as the saffron infuses. Then boil rapidly for about 1 minute to reduce somewhat and whisk in the remaining 1½ oz (40 g) chilled butter cut into cubes – add these one at a time. The sauce should now be glossy and pale golden and speckled with the deeper golden saffron threads.

To serve, place a shallow nest of spinach on each of 4 warmed plates. Carefully lift the fish steaks out of their parcels, keeping their vegetables intact on the top, and place them in the spinach nests. Lace each steak with the sauce, surround with a few tiny boiled new potatoes and serve immediately.

Crab claws with chilli

A spicy dish from the Far East. If you wish you can serve it with accompaniments such as bamboo shoots, fried seaweed or rice.

Serves 4

2 medium crabs

Sunflower oil

1 bunch spring onions, trimmed and sliced on the diagonal, including all the good green parts

4 cloves garlic, peeled and finely chopped

1–2 fresh red chillies, de-seeded and finely chopped

10 fl oz (300 ml) water

1 tablespoon light soy sauce

1 teaspoon sugar

1 inch (2.5 cm) piece fresh root ginger, peeled and grated

Boiled rice to serve

If the crabs are live, boil them for 5 minutes and drain well. Detach the claws and crack them with a rolling pin or the back of a cleaver. The main shell can be reserved for stock or soup.

Heat a large wok, add the oil and swirl it around, then stir-fry the spring onions, garlic and chillies for 1 minute. Now add the water, soy sauce, sugar and ginger, bring to the boil and cook for 1 more minute. Add the cracked crab claws and continue simmering for a further 5 minutes as their flesh absorbs the spicy flavours of the stock.

To serve, arrange the claws on plain boiled rice and strain the stock over.

Stuffed baby squid

Small squid are tender and fabulous for grilling or barbecuing. Yes, I know they're strange and messy-looking, but if you haven't already tried them on a Portuguese beach, I promise that when you cook these you are in for a pleasant surprise. If you're uncertain about preparing them, ask your fishmonger to do the job for you.

Serves 2

1–1½ lb (450–750 g) small squid

Herb Oil for cooking (see page 214)

Lemon wedges to serve

Stuffing:

4 ripe tomatoes, skinned, de-seeded and finely chopped

1–2 cloves garlic, peeled and very finely chopped

2 oz (50 g) breadcrumbs

½ tablespoon chopped fresh herbs (fennel leaves, basil, dill or oregano as available and to taste)

Pinch of salt

Plenty of freshly ground black pepper

Combine all the stuffing ingredients thoroughly in a bowl.

Prepare the squid – pull out the head and innards, skin the squid sacs under cold running water and pat dry with kitchen paper. Chop off the tentacles taking care to remove the hard inedible mouth (or beak), slice them finely and add these to the stuffing ingredients. Now stuff the squid sacs fairly loosely (or they may burst during cooking) and secure with wooden cocktail sticks. This preparation can be done well in advance if you wish.

When you are ready to cook, light the barbecue and get it good and hot, or pre-heat the grill; oil the rack. Brush the squid well with Herb Oil and barbecue or grill for about 15 minutes, turning them for even cooking and basting occasionally. Serve immediately with wedges of lemon.

Salmon with lemon grass

This is a simple yet intriguing way of presenting and serving large whole fish, particularly salmon or large trout. Lemon grass (see page 17) infuses the dish with an exquisite lemony floral flavour. A friend's suggestion of first slicing the fish into steaks, then re-assembling them into the original fish shape before wrapping in aluminium foil for baking, both makes a beautiful centrepiece for the table and overcomes the fiddly problem of serving fish off the bone. Just lift out a cutlet for each guest, spooning over a little of the aromatic cooking juices and offering dishes of boiled tiny new potatoes and lightly herbed salad leaves alongside.

Serves 4–6

1 × 2½–3 lb (1.25–1.4 kg) wild salmon

A little oil or butter for greasing

Pinch of salt

Freshly ground black pepper

2–3 sticks lemon grass, upper and outer leaves discarded, and finely sliced on the diagonal

2 oz (50 g) butter

4–6 tablespoons Pouilly-Fuissé (or other white wine or dry vermouth)

Green fennel or dill fronds to garnish

A little extra butter and whipping cream (optional)

Pre-heat the oven to gas mark 5, 375°F (190°C).

Gut and scale the salmon or ask your fishmonger to do this for you. Wash under cold running water, making sure that the belly cavity is thoroughly cleaned out and free of blood on the backbone. Pat dry with kitchen paper. Using strong kitchen scissors, cut off the fins. Snap out the gills. Lightly grease a double-thickness sheet of aluminium foil large enough to parcel the fish.

Put the salmon on a work-surface or large board and, using a good sharp knife and starting from the head end, slice the fish into 4–6 1½–2 inch steaks each (3–5 cm) thick. Lightly season the steaks on each side with salt and pepper and put the whole fish (including the head and tail) back together again on the prepared foil. Push slivers of lemon grass and tiny knobs of butter between each steak. Season the fish again all over with salt and pepper and bring up the sides of the foil to form an open parcel. Splash the wine all over, then seal the foil to make a loose parcel. Put the parcel on a baking sheet or in a large roasting tin and bake in the oven for about 25–30 minutes. When the flesh is opaque and eases away from the backbone, the fish is cooked.

Transfer the parcelled fish to an oval serving platter, peel back the foil and strew with green fennel fronds or dill. Spoon over the delicious cooking juices as you serve each steak.

Alternatively, before taking the fish to the table, drain off the cooking juices into a saucepan, bring to the boil and finish with a nut of butter or swirl of whipping cream. Hand this sauce separately.

My hearty seafood stew

An easily prepared stew using a variety of the freshest fish you can find. You can choose from among the many firm white fish available, such as monkfish, catfish and swordfish, and add your preferred shellfish: these can range from cheap and delicious cockles and mussels to the more expensive Dublin Bay prawns or a small sliced crawfish. Serve with boiled potatoes or lots of crusty bread.

Serves 4–6

1½ lb (700 g) firm white fish fillets

About 1 lb (450 g) fresh unshelled prawns or squid

15 fl oz (400 ml) fish stock

About 2 lb (900 g) mussels or small clams

2–3 tablespoons olive oil

1 medium onion, peeled and finely chopped

3 fat cloves garlic, peeled and chopped

1 green pepper, de-seeded and finely chopped

1 small red chilli, de-seeded and finely chopped

1 × 14 oz (400 g) tin tomatoes, chopped, with their juice

2 teaspoons tomato purée

5 fl oz (150 ml) white wine

Pinch of salt

Freshly ground black pepper

1 tablespoon single cream (optional)

Finely chopped parsley to garnish

First prepare the fish. Check that no bones remain, wash it, pat dry and cut into neat bite-sized pieces. Set aside. If you are using prawns, shell them and reserve the shells: add the shells to the fish stock and simmer for 10 minutes to strengthen its flavour. Strain and set aside. If you are using squid, prepare it as described on page 183, then slice it into ¼ inch (5 mm) rings. Steam open the mussels or clams and add their juices to the stock. Discard the shells but reserve 8 mussels or a handful of clams in the shell to garnish the finished dish.

Heat the olive oil in a very large heavy-bottomed saucepan and gently fry the onion, garlic, green pepper and chilli in it for about 4–5 minutes. Add the tomatoes and their juice, the tomato purée, fish stock and the white wine. Simmer gently for 30 minutes to reduce somewhat. Bearing in mind the fact that your fish stock is already seasoned, lightly season to taste with salt and pepper. Remember that fish also contains its own salt.

Add the fish pieces and squid (if using) to the stock and poach them very gently for 4 minutes, then add the prawns (if using), the mussels or clams and the cream (if using) and heat through for a further 2 minutes.

To serve, use a slotted spoon to transfer the fish and shellfish to warmed large shallow soup bowls or large dinner plates. Spoon over all the stock, garnish with the reserved mussels or clams and sprinkle with chopped parsley.

Vegetables

Fiery three-bean chilli

In this meatless 'chilli con carne' the beef is replaced with a colourful combination of beans. It's a versatile recipe; and you need have no compunction in using tinned beans (an excellent store-cupboard standby) to avoid the lengthy and varying soaking and cooking times required by dried beans. Serve the chilli on plain boiled rice.

Serves 4–6

3–4 tablespoons good-quality olive oil

2 large onions, peeled and chopped

3 fat cloves garlic, peeled and chopped

1 red pepper, de-seeded and sliced

2–3 fresh red chillies (according to taste), de-seeded and finely chopped

2 × 14 oz (400 g) tins tomatoes

1 glass red wine

Pinch of salt

Freshly ground black pepper

1 × 14 oz (400 g) tin red kidney beans, drained and rinsed

1 × 14 oz (400 g) tin flageolet beans, drained and rinsed

1 × 14 oz (400 g) tin white kidney or butter beans, drained and rinsed

4–6 oz (110–175 g) mushrooms, quartered

In a large heavy pan heat 2–3 tablespoons of the olive oil and add the onions, garlic, red pepper and preferred number of chillies. Cook them very gently, without browning, for about 10 minutes or until they are totally soft. Now chop the tomatoes and add them and their juice to the pan together with the red wine. Season with a little salt and plenty of freshly ground black pepper. Heat until barely simmering. Add the beans and stir them gently in. Simmer for 20 minutes. In a separate pan quickly sear the mushrooms in the remaining 1 tablespoon or so of olive oil and add these to the chilli 5 minutes before the end of the cooking time.

Galette of aubergines and pasta with tomato and basil sauce

If you cannot get fresh basil for this recipe, don't substitute dried basil – its flavour is nothing compared with that of the pungent fresh leaves. Instead, use dried oregano which is more acceptable in this dish. A 7 inch (18 cm) spring-sided cake tin is helpful when it comes to turning out the galette. Serve with crusty bread and a crisp green salad.

Serves 4

4–5 medium aubergines

Salt

1 medium onion, peeled and finely chopped

2 fat cloves garlic, peeled and crushed

Good-quality olive oil

1 lb (450 g) ripe tomatoes, skinned and de-seeded, or 1 × 14 oz (400 g) tin tomatoes

1 tablespoon tomato purée

½ tablespoon chopped fresh basil leaves or a little dried oregano

1 glass red wine

1 strip lemon rind

Freshly ground black pepper

1 lb (450 g) lasagne

Butter for glazing

1 × 5 oz (150 g) carton fromage frais or natural yoghurt

Sprig of fresh basil to garnish (optional)

Slice the aubergines into thinnish rounds, sprinkle with salt and leave for 30 minutes to enable them to exude their bitter juices. Rinse them well and pat dry with kitchen paper.

Meanwhile, make the tomato sauce. In a heavy-bottomed pan, gently soften the onion and garlic in 1 tablespoon olive oil over a gentle heat. Now add the tomatoes (and their juice if using the tinned variety), the tomato purée, basil, wine and lemon rind and season to taste with salt and pepper. Simmer for at least 20 minutes or until the sauce is reduced and thick. Remove the lemon rind and discard. Set the sauce aside.

Cook the lasagne in batches in a large wide pan according to the instructions on the packet until *al dente*. Remove each batch from the pan with slotted spoons, plunge into cold water and drain on clean teatowels.

Pre-heat the oven to gas mark 4, 350°F (180°C).

Heat about ¼ inch (5 mm) olive oil in a large frying-pan and fry the aubergine slices in batches until brown on both sides, replenishing the oil as necessary. Drain each batch thoroughly on kitchen paper. Use a scrap of butter to grease a 7 inch (18 cm) spring-sided cake tin. Line it with a layer of aubergine slices. Spread the base with a little tomato sauce and a little fromage frais or yoghurt. Then add a layer of pasta. Repeat the layers, ending with a layer of aubergine. Cover with a sheet of aluminium foil and press down lightly. Bake in the oven for 45 minutes.

Meanwhile, put the remaining sauce into a food processor or liquidiser and whizz until smooth. Re-heat and add a little of the remaining fromage frais or yoghurt to taste.

Allow the galette to cool slightly, then invert the tin on to a warm serving plate and release the spring and base. Serve warm, garnished with a sprig of basil if available, and hand the sauce separately.

Celeriac, pine nut and goat's cheese strudels with watercress sauce

These light, melt-in-the-mouth strudels are set on a pool of fresh-tasting watercress sauce. For a special main course, make an attractive nouvelle *kind of plate arrangement with the strudels sliced on the diagonal, punctuated with asparagus or whole steamed baby leeks and pretty bundles of julienned vegetables. It is quite a rich dish, so put a bowl of tiny new potatoes or noodles on the table as well. It looks very impressive, but in fact the preparation is simple.*

Strudels are very easy to make if you use prepared filo pastry. All sorts of vegetable combinations can be used instead of the one suggested: for instance, herbed cabbage and apple; or cheese, spring onions and soured cream; or celery and walnut.

Serves 2

2 sheets filo pastry, thawed if frozen

3 oz (75 g) melted butter

1½ lb (700 g) celeriac, peeled and coarsely grated

6–8 oz (175–225 g) hard goat's cheese, crumbled, rind discarded

4 oz (110 g) pine nuts

1 tablespoon chopped fresh herbs (such as sage with a hint of rosemary)

Freshly ground black pepper

Sauce:

2–3 bunches watercress, tough stalks removed

5 fl oz (150 ml) Greek-style yoghurt

5 fl oz (150 ml) whipping cream

Juice of 1 lemon

1–2 cloves garlic, peeled and chopped

Pinch of salt

Freshly ground black pepper

Pre-heat the oven to gas mark 4, 350°F (180°C).

Spread out 1 oblong sheet of the filo pastry and brush it very lightly with a little melted butter. Cover with half the celeriac, leaving a 1 inch (2.5 cm) border of pastry all around it. Sprinkle with half the crumbled cheese, pine nuts and herbs and season with a grinding of pepper. Fold in the 2 long edges, then fold over the edge nearest to you and carefully roll up the strudel. You may find the rolling easier if you first place the pastry on a clean teatowel. When you get to the end of the roll, seal it to the open flap with a little melted butter. Use a palette knife to transfer the strudel to a baking sheet. Repeat the process with the remaining ingredients.

Brush the strudels very lightly with melted butter, cover loosely with buttered greaseproof paper and bake in the oven for 20 minutes. Then remove the paper, brush again with butter, and bake for a final 10–15 minutes or until golden and crisp.

Meanwhile, make the sauce. Blanch the watercress for 30 seconds in boiling water, drain, plunge into cold water to refresh, and drain again. Pat dry with kitchen paper. Put the watercress into a food processor or liquidiser with the remaining sauce ingredients and whizz until you have a smooth, speckled sauce. Carefully cut the strudels slightly on the diagonal into 2–3 inch (5–7.5 cm) slices and serve on the watercress sauce.

Cauliflower cheese

I make no excuse for including my version of this favourite dish – it is simply one of the best dishes in the world. Some rather worldly and sophisticated Swiss guests at my island home wanted it again and again – when I had thought they would be thrilled with my lobster quenelles and so on. I think it must have that indefinable timeless appeal of a simple but winning combination of flavours with the cook's own touch – in my case, of course, garlic and onion. The dish is actually baked, so be more than usually careful in the first place not to overcook the cauliflower. Serve with baked jacket potatoes.

Serves 4

1 fine large cauliflower, including all the good green leaves

Salt

3 oz (75 g) butter

1 medium onion, peeled and finely chopped

About 1 pint (570 ml) milk

2 cloves garlic, peeled and crushed

2 oz (50 g) flour

8 oz (225 g) Cheddar cheese, grated

Freshly ground black pepper

Pre-heat the oven to gas mark 6, 400°F (200°C).

Break the cauliflower into florets and boil in lightly salted water, with all the good green leaves, for about 5 minutes; it should be *al dente*. Drain the cauliflower and reserve the cooking water.

Meanwhile, make the sauce. Melt 2 oz (50 g) of the butter in a saucepan and gently fry the onion until it is very soft but not brown. While the onion is frying, heat the milk in another pan. Add the garlic to the onion in the final stages of its frying, stir, then stir in the flour and cook for 30 seconds. Remove the pan from the heat and pour in the heated milk all at once. Return to the heat, stirring all the time to achieve a very thick creamy sauce and adding 6–7 oz (175–200 g) of the cheese as you go until it has all melted.

Now add about 5 fl oz (150 ml) of the reserved cauliflower water to thin down the sauce a little and add flavour. Season to taste with salt and pepper.

Use the remaining 1 oz (25 g) butter to grease a shallow earthenware baking dish. Line it with the cooked green cauliflower leaves, add the florets and coat with all the sauce. Sprinkle with the remaining 1–2 oz (25–50 g) cheese and bake in the oven for about 20 minutes.

My hearty seafood stew (page 185), and Salmon with lemon grass (page 184)

Braised celery and chestnuts with creamy cheese sauce

A savoury dish with a tinge of sweetness and a haunting sauce. Serve the tender celery hearts on a bed of nutty brown rice and scatter generously with chopped celery leaves to brighten up the dish as it is rather pale in appearance.

Serves 4

2 large or 4 small heads celery

1 × 15 oz (425 g) tin whole chestnuts in water

1 pint (570 ml) vegetable stock

4 oz (110 g) cream cheese

1–2 egg yolks

Pinch of salt

Freshly ground white pepper

Boiled brown rice to serve

Pre-heat the oven to gas mark 5, 375°F (190°C).

Remove the tough outer stalks from the celery heads, trim the tough base and cut off the upper part of the stalks so that you are left with nice firm white celery hearts measuring about 6 inches (15 cm) long. Reserve the green celery leaves to garnish the dish and use the remaining stalks and trimmings for stock or soup. If you have 2 large celery hearts, cut them in half lengthways; if you have 4 smaller hearts, leave them whole.

Put the celery into a flameproof casserole, add the chestnuts with their water and cover with the stock. Bring to simmering point on the top of the stove, then cover and braise in the oven for about 40 minutes or until the celery is really tender – test it with a sharp knife or skewer. The celery will be a rather dull buff colour by now, but don't worry because soon it will be coated in a beautiful creamy sauce. Using a perforated spoon, transfer the celery and half the chestnuts to a warmed dish and keep warm.

Now put the cream cheese into a food processor or liquidiser, add 10 fl oz (300 ml) of the slightly cooled cooking liquid and the remaining chestnuts and whizz for about 45 seconds or until smooth. Pour this mixture into a saucepan and heat gently. Put the egg yolks into a small basin and beat them a little, adding 1 tablespoon of the warm sauce and beating gently to incorporate. Add 1–2 tablespoons more of the sauce and stir, then draw the saucepan off the heat and tip in the egg yolk mixture and stir well to

Fried rice with brussels sprouts, eggs and nuts (page 211), Gougère of creamy young vegetables (page 208), and Slow-roast onions osborne with chilled chickpea and cashew salad (page 200)

incorporate. Return the pan to a low heat (or use a double saucepan) and stir all the time as the sauce heats through and begins to thicken. Do not allow the sauce to boil as this will cause the eggs to curdle. When the sauce coats the back of your wooden spoon, it is about the right consistency. Taste it and season with salt and pepper. If you wish, you can add a little more of the cooking liquid. Arrange the celery hearts and whole chestnuts on the boiled rice, pour over the sauce, scatter with lots of chopped celery leaves and serve immediately.

Chicory, leek and sage flan

The slightly bitter-tasting heads of white chicory are set in a wheel shape on a purée of leeks in a cheese pastry flan and covered with a sprinkling of sage and a creamy cheese custard. Serve with noodles and grilled field mushrooms.

Serves 4–6

4 fat heads chicory, trimmed

1½ lb (700 g) leeks (trimmed weight)

2–3 oz (50–75 g) unsalted butter

3–4 oz (75–110 g) Cheddar cheese, grated

2 teaspoons finely chopped fresh sage leaves

2 eggs, beaten

5 fl oz (150 ml) milk

5 fl oz (150 ml) single cream

Pinch of salt

Freshly ground black pepper

Cheese Pastry:

1½ oz (40 g) white Flora

1½ oz (40 g) butter

6 oz (175 g) flour

Pinch of salt

3 oz (75 g) Cheddar cheese, finely grated

Ice-cold water to mix

First make the pastry in the usual way, rubbing the fat into the sieved flour and salt with your finger tips (which should be cool), raising your hands well above the bowl as you do so to let in plenty of air. When the mixture resembles fine breadcrumbs, add the cheese, making sure that it is thoroughly distributed, then sprinkle with ice-cold water – a little at a time – and mix and draw together quickly and lightly with a cool knife blade to form a soft ball. Cover the pastry and leave it to rest in a cool place for 30 minutes.

Now cook the chicory in boiling water for 10–15 minutes or until tender. Drain and leave to cool a little. Meanwhile, trim, wash and thinly slice the leeks, including the good green parts. Melt the butter in a large heavy pan, add the leeks, cover with a piece of butter paper and cook over a gentle heat, stirring from time to time, for 20–30 minutes or until they are absolutely soft and creamy. All the preparation so far can be done some time in advance if you wish.

When you are ready to cook, pre-heat the oven to gas mark 4, 350°F (180°C). Roll out the pastry and use it to line a 10 inch (25 cm) flan dish. Prick the base several times with a fork and bake in the oven for 15 minutes. Remove the flan case from the oven and set aside. Turn up the oven to gas mark 5, 375°F (190°C).

Spread the leeks over the base of the flan case. Carefully slice each head of chicory in half lengthways and arrange the halves on the leeks so that they resemble the spokes of a wheel, pointed ends to the centre. Fill in the gaps with grated cheese. Scatter the sage all over. Lightly whisk together the eggs, milk and cream; season with a little salt and pepper and pour into the flan case. Bake in the oven for 35–40 minutes or until the custard is firm and golden.

Cheese, leek and sage pudding

A comforting old-fashioned nursery kind of dish which has a delicious squidgy sort of fondue middle and a golden-domed cheesy crust. Because of its soft pudding texture, I like to serve it warm accompanied by lightly cooked broccoli, cauliflower, runner beans or carrots. It is quick to prepare, and an oblong baking dish makes the arrangement of the bread slices easier. You can use wholemeal bread instead of white if you wish, but the pudding will not be as light.

Serves 4

2 oz (50 g) butter plus extra for greasing

1 lb (450 g) white part of leeks, washed and finely chopped

3 eggs

10 fl oz (300 ml) milk

5 fl oz (150 ml) cream

Pinch of salt

Freshly ground black pepper

About 10 slices good white bread, crusts removed

8 oz (225 g) Cheddar cheese, grated

1–2 teaspoons dried sage

Pre-heat the oven to gas mark 4, 350°F (180°C).

In a large heavy-bottomed pan melt the butter over a gentle heat, add the leeks and cook them very slowly without browning for about 10 minutes or until they are totally soft. Set aside. Lightly grease a baking dish with butter.

In a shallow bowl lightly whisk together the eggs, milk and cream and season to taste with salt and pepper. Dip the slices of bread into this custard and use them to line the base of the dish. Sprinkle some of the cheese on to each slice, scatter with a little sage and cover with half the cooked leeks. Repeat the layers and finish with a layer of bread scattered generously with cheese. Bake in the oven for about 45 minutes or until well risen, firm, golden-crusted and domed. Serve warm.

Marrow and thyme croustade

What to do with that surfeit of marrows? The marrow has such a pleasant delicate flavour which is often overwhelmed when baked and stuffed, and it tends to be watery and difficult to serve in an interesting way. Here is a delightful recipe which transforms this vegetable into a luscious dish for a dinner party: serve with a colourful selection of steamed vegetables and tiny potatoes. Avoid using very large marrows – over 2½ lb (1.25 kg) – which are far too soft and watery for this recipe.

Serves 4–6

2 oz (50 g) unsalted butter

2 medium onions, peeled and very finely chopped

2 lb (900 g) marrow, peeled, fibrous centre removed and cut into 1 inch (2.5 cm) cubes

3 teaspoons chopped fresh thyme

3–4 tablespoons fromage frais

Pinch of salt

Freshly ground white pepper

Base:

8 oz (225 g) fresh wholemeal breadcrumbs

6 oz (175 g) Cheddar cheese, grated

2 oz (50 g) butter

1 teaspoon fresh thyme

4 oz (110 g) pine nuts

In a large heavy saucepan melt the butter and gently fry the onions until they are soft and transparent, but do not let them brown. Add the marrow and thyme and stir gently to mix with the onions and coat with the butter. Cover and cook on a very low heat for at least 20 minutes, stirring occasionally, until the marrow is tender. Remove the lid, turn up the heat slightly and cook for a further 5 minutes or so until most of the marrow juices have evaporated – stir very gently at this stage so that you don't break up the cubes of marrow.

Meanwhile, pre-heat the oven to gas mark 7, 425°F (220°C), and prepare the base. Reserve 1 oz (25 g) each of the breadcrumbs and cheese and fork the butter into the remaining breadcrumbs. Mix in the rest of the ingredients (apart from the reserved breadcrumbs and cheese) and press into a lightly buttered loose-bottomed 9–10 inch (23–25 cm) cake or flan tin. Push a little of the base up the sides of the tin to make a slight rim. Bake in the oven for about 15–20 minutes. Remove from the oven and allow to cool slightly, then slide the base on to an attractive warmed serving platter and keep warm.

By now the thyme-scented marrow should be moist with just a very little liquid left in the pan. Pre-heat the grill. Carefully stir the fromage frais into the marrow, season to taste with salt and pepper, then tip the mixture on to the base. Scatter with the reserved breadcrumbs and cheese and flash under the grill to brown. Serve immediately.

Mushroom creams

For these you need really huge – 3–4 inch (7.5–10 cm) diameter – flat mushrooms with dark healthy gills. If you are lucky enough to find large shaggy parasols (as I do on an island near my home in the Isles of Scilly), these would be very good too, but do consult a good illustrated guide when collecting wild mushrooms. Serve the Mushroom Creams with a little plain boiled rice or braised celery and follow with a green salad.

Serves 2

2 very large flat mushrooms

Freshly ground black pepper

2 oz (50 g) butter

1 egg and 1 egg yolk

4 tablespoons cream or fromage frais

2 oz (50 g) Parmesan cheese, grated

Pinch of salt

Chervil sprigs to garnish

Pre-heat the oven to gas mark 6, 400°F (200°C).

Wipe the mushrooms very well and, if you have gathered them in the wild, inspect the gills for insects. Carefully cut off the stem of each mushroom, chop finely and sprinkle back into the inverted caps. Season with pepper, then distribute just a few little scraps of butter in each cap. Cut out 2 sheets of aluminium foil each large enough to parcel a mushroom comfortably and lightly butter the centre of each. Put a mushroom, gill side up, on each of the sheets, draw up the sides and crinkle them together to make a loose purse-shaped parcel. Place on a baking sheet and cook for 15 minutes.

Remove the parcels from the oven and open them. Carefully spoon out the dark mushroom liquid which will have exuded from each cap – there should be about 2 tablespoons – put it into a small saucepan and set aside. Close the parcels again, turn down the oven to gas mark 4, 350°F (180°C), and continue to cook the mushrooms for a further 30 minutes or until they are tender. Take the mushroom parcels out of the oven again, remove the chopped stems from the caps and add these and their juices to the juices in the saucepan. Keep the mushroom caps warm. Add 2–3 tablespoons water to the saucepan, boil to reduce, strain, then whisk in a little knob of butter – there should be about 2 tablespoons dark glossy sauce. Keep warm.

Now pre-heat the grill. Mix together the egg, egg yolk, cream or fromage blanc and 1½ oz (40 g) of the Parmesan cheese. Pour into a small saucepan and cook very very gently over a low heat, stirring all the time, until the mixture becomes creamy and curdy and is almost setting. Add a little salt to taste. Pour this mixture into the mushroom caps and dust with the remaining ½ oz (10 g) Parmesan. Flash under the grill for 30 seconds until golden.

To serve, set each mushroom cream on a warmed plate, trickle the sauce around and decorate with a sprig of chervil.

Porcini with spaghetti

Dried porcini (ceps) have a wonderful savoury flavour. These mushrooms are expensive, but for this dish I buy a packet of broken pieces which cost considerably less. Italian food shops, delicatessens and some supermarkets stock them, and they are most useful to keep in your store-cupboard (see page 11) for adding to soups, sauces and all manner of dishes. You can, of course, use whole dried porcini if your budget allows.

Serves 4

8 oz (225 g) dried *porcini* pieces

Sea salt

4 tablespoons extra virgin olive oil

12 oz (350 g) spaghetti

2–3 fat cloves garlic, peeled and finely chopped

1 bunch spring onions, trimmed and white parts finely chopped (reserve green tops to garnish)

3 tablespoons finely chopped fresh mint

Freshly ground black pepper

Put the *porcini* into a basin, cover with hot (not boiling) water, cover and leave to soak for about 15 minutes.

Meanwhile, bring a large pan of salted water to the boil and add a drop of oil – this will prevent the spaghetti sticking. Put in the spaghetti and boil for about 8 minutes or until just tender. (If you are using fresh pasta, it will take only 2–3 minutes.)

Drain the *porcini*, reserving the dark liquid. Squeeze or pat dry with kitchen paper. Strain the liquid through a sieve lined with kitchen paper to remove any pieces of grit. Heat a wok or large heavy frying-pan and add the oil. Add the garlic and white parts of the spring onions and cook gently for 2 minutes. Then add the *porcini* and 2 tablespoons of the mint and continue cooking for 2 more minutes.

Meanwhile, drain the spaghetti, return it to its warm pan and keep warm for a moment or two.

Now add 3–4 tablespoons of the reserved *porcini* soaking liquid to the wok, season with salt and pepper to taste and heat through. Pour the contents of the wok over the spaghetti and use 2 large-pronged spaghetti forks to urge the *porcini* around all the strands.

Tip into a large shallow serving dish and scatter with the reserved 1 tablespoon mint and a few chopped spring onion greens. Serve immediately with chilled wine.

Slow-roast onions Osborne served on a chilled chickpea and cashew salad

Sounds like an explosive combination, doesn't it? But slow-roasting whole unpeeled onions makes them wonderfully sweet and creamy-tasting, and in this recipe each is served with a melting nugget of butter flavoured with fresh orange, coriander and walnuts. The onions are brought to the table piping hot in the centre of a circle of chilled chickpea salad bordered by an outer circle of sliced tomatoes: a colourful and unusual dish which would be ideal for a meatless supper party.

Serves 4

12 oz (350 g) chickpeas

4 large firm Spanish onions with good intact skins

4 oz (110 g) walnuts, ground or chopped

4 tablespoons finely chopped fresh coriander or parsley, plus a few whole leaves to garnish

4 oz (110 g) butter or polyunsaturated margarine

Juice of 2 oranges plus 2 teaspoons grated orange rind

2–3 tablespoons tahini

2–3 tablespoons Greek yoghurt

1 fat clove garlic, crushed

Juice of ½ lemon

Pinch of salt

Freshly ground black pepper

4 oz (110 g) cashew nuts

4 large ripe tomatoes

Soak the chickpeas in cold water overnight. Drain, then simmer in fresh water for about 2½ hours or until tender. Drain and set aside.

Pre-heat the oven to gas mark 3, 325°F (170°C). Wipe the onions and stand them upright in a roasting tin. If they are wobbly, stand each one in a little cradle of crumpled aluminium foil to keep it steady. Bake the onions in the oven for about 1½ hours or until tender right through; to test for this, push a thin skewer down through the top.

While the onions are roasting, beat together the ground or chopped walnuts, coriander or parsley and butter or margarine, gradually adding the juice of 1 orange and 2 teaspoons grated rind to make a smooth mixture.

In another bowl lightly whisk together the tahini, yoghurt, garlic, lemon juice and remaining orange juice to make a fairly stiff dressing. Season with a pinch of salt and freshly ground black pepper to taste and stir in the whole cashew nuts and chickpeas.

Slice the tomatoes. On each of 4 plates arrange an outer circle of tomatoes and then an inner circle of the chickpea salad, garnished with a few whole coriander or parsley leaves. Place a hot onion in the centre of each plate. Cut a 1 inch (2.5 cm) deep cross on the top of each onion and peel back the outer skin and one or two of the inner layers. Put a nugget of the walnut butter into each onion and serve straight away, providing a spoon for the onion and a fork for the delicious surrounding salad.

Spinach, feta and tomato pie

You can use fresh or frozen prepared spinach for this dish. I like to make it with wild sea beet which is extremely prolific around some coastal areas and has a stronger wilder sort of taste than cultivated spinach but looks very much the same.

The pie has a gorgeous gungy middle and is rather filling, so I think it is best served simply with a selection of salads. It also makes delicious cold picnic fare.

Serves 4

Spinach Filling:

1 lb (450 g) spinach, washed and tough ribs removed, or 8 oz (225 g) frozen spinach, thawed

2 oz (50 g) butter

1 medium onion, peeled and very finely chopped

10 fl oz (300 ml) milk

2 oz (50 g) flour

Pinch of salt

Freshly ground black pepper

4 tomatoes, skinned and cut into thick slices

1 tablespoon sunflower oil

Pinch of salt

Freshly ground black pepper

Pinch of sugar (optional)

Flour for dusting

15 oz (425 g) frozen puff pastry, thawed

1 small egg, beaten

4 oz (110 g) feta cheese, crumbled

First prepare the Spinach Filling. If you are using fresh spinach, put it in a large heavy pan and cook for about 8 minutes in just the water that clings to the leaves after rinsing. Drain and squeeze out as much moisture as you can: an effective method is to place the spinach in a clean teatowel and twist. Chop the spinach roughly. If you are using thawed frozen spinach, drain it and chop it roughly after thawing. Set aside.

Now make the sauce. Melt the butter in a small heavy pan, add the onion and cook gently for about 10 minutes or until very soft, but do not allow it to brown. Meanwhile, heat the milk in another pan. Sprinkle the flour into the onion and stir over a gentle heat for 2 minutes. Take off the heat and add the hot milk all at once. Stir well, return the pan to the heat and continue stirring until a really thick white sauce results. Season to taste with salt and pepper and stir in the spinach. You should have a stiff creamy mixture. Keep warm.

In another small pan gently fry the tomatoes in the oil until their juices are released and they are soft and *just* hold their shape. Season with salt and pepper, add a little sugar if they are rather on the tasteless side and keep warm.

Pre-heat the oven to gas mark 8, 450°F (230°C).

On a cool floured surface, roll out the puff pastry to form an oblong measuring roughly 9 × 6 inches (23 × 15 cm) – it should be ⅛ inch (3 mm) thick. Place on a cool baking sheet and leave in a cool place to relax for 10 minutes, then brush lightly with beaten egg and bake in the oven for about 15 minutes or until risen and golden-brown. Allow to cool slightly and carefully slice the top of the risen pastry and set aside – this will form the lid of the pie. Scoop out a few of the uncooked soft layers of pastry from the base and return the base to the oven for a further 6–7 minutes or until it has cooked through. Remove from the oven and allow to subside and cool a little – it should have an outer puffed-up rim and a firmish base, rather like a giant vol-au-vent.

Turn the oven down to gas mark 2, 300°F (150°C). Tip the spinach mixture into the pastry base, spread it evenly, top with the crumbled feta cheese and add the tomatoes and their juices. Return the puff pastry lid to the pie and warm the whole dish through in the oven for about 10 minutes. To serve cut into four at the table.

Spinach pancakes

Once you have made the creamy spinach filling for the pancakes, this delicious light supper main course can be easily assembled. Serve with grilled tomato halves and mushrooms, and a potato gratin.

Serves 4–6

Batter:

2–3 oz (50–75 g) plain flour

Pinch of salt

1 egg and 1 egg yolk, lightly beaten

7 fl oz (200 ml) milk

1 oz (25 g) butter, melted

A little sunflower oil for frying

1 quantity Spinach Filling (see page 202)

3–4 tablespoons whipping cream

4 oz (110 g) Gruyère or Cheddar cheese, grated

To make the pancake batter, sift the flour and salt into a mixing bowl. Make a well in the centre, add the egg and egg yolk and stir, drawing the flour in gradually as you do so. Beat in the milk a little at a time to make a smooth thinnish batter: adjust the amount of flour and milk slightly as necessary. Leave the batter to stand for at least 10 minutes. Just before you fry the pancakes, whisk in the melted butter.

Heat a heavy 7 inch (18 cm) frying-pan, add just enough oil to coat the base and fry the pancakes in the usual way, turning them over half-way through the cooking time. This quantity of batter should make 6 pancakes. As each one is cooked, stack them on a plate and keep warm.

When you are ready to assemble the dish, pre-heat the oven to gas mark 8, 450°F (230°C). Spread equal quantities of the spinach mixture on each of the pancakes, roll them up and arrange them in a lightly buttered baking dish. Trickle a little whipping cream over each one, then scatter with the grated cheese. Bake in the oven for 10–15 minutes or until golden-brown, or finish under a hot grill.

Sarah's parsnip, parsley, thyme and onion loaf

This loaf has a delicate fragrant flavour and is good served hot or cold, but I prefer it sliced warm with crusty bread and a 'sour' leaf salad, like endive, chicory or raw spinach with a good vinaigrette dressing.

Serves 4–6

1 lb (450 g) parsnips, peeled and cut into chunks

1 large onion, peeled and finely chopped

1 oz (25 g) butter

1 tablespoon soured cream

2 eggs, beaten

3 tablespoons chopped parsley

1–2 good handfuls breadcrumbs

1 tablespoon chopped fresh thyme

Pinch of sea salt

Freshly ground black pepper

Pre-heat the oven to gas mark 4, 350°F (180°C).

Boil the parsnips in water until tender. Meanwhile, in a small pan, cook the onion in the butter over a gentle heat until soft but not brown. Strain the parsnips and mash vigorously with the soured cream. Add the onion and remaining ingredients and mix well.

Put the mixture into a lightly buttered 1 lb (450 g) loaf tin, cover with aluminium foil and bake in the oven for 45 minutes or until the loaf is firm. Test whether it is thoroughly cooked by piercing with a skewer or knitting needle; if it comes out clean, the loaf is ready. Allow to cool a little, then invert the tin on to a warm platter to serve.

Crispy pancake rolls

*When you are cooking a batch of pancakes, make extra ones and store in the refrigerator –
they keep well for at least a week. Then you can easily prepare these crispy rolls for a light
main course, served with fried rice and braised lettuce or Chinese leaves. No sauce or
anything special in the way of accompaniment is required, except perhaps a sprinkling or
two of soy sauce.*

Serves 4

8 pancakes (see page 204)

1 tablespoon clear honey

Sunflower oil

Dark soy sauce

Filling:

1 inch (2.5 cm) piece fresh root ginger, peeled and finely chopped

1 bunch spring onions, trimmed and sliced on the diagonal, including all the
good green parts

1 fat clove garlic, peeled and finely chopped

2 sticks celery, finely sliced

4 oz (110 g) bean sprouts

4 oz (110 g) shredded root vegetable (such as young turnip or carrot)

1 handful lettuce or spinach ribbons

Freshly ground black pepper

A little flour-and-water paste

Make sure that you have warm plates ready and all your ingredients
prepared before you begin to cook.

Spread each pancake with a very little honey, then sprinkle all over with
soy sauce.

Heat a wok or frying-pan, add 1 tablespoon oil and swirl around, then add
all the vegetable ingredients except the lettuce or spinach and stir-fry for 1
minute only. Add the lettuce or spinach for the final few seconds and season
with pepper. (You will not need salt because the soy sauce is salty.)

Heap 1 or 2 tablespoons of the vegetables in the centre of each pancake.
Fold in the sides then roll up fairly tightly. Use the flour-and-water paste to
secure.

Wipe out the wok or frying-pan with kitchen paper, add about 2 inches (5 cm) of fresh oil and heat. Fry the pancake rolls in batches for about 5 minutes, turning once. Drain each batch well on kitchen paper and keep warm until all the rolls are cooked, then serve.

Savoury oat, cheese and onion roast

Everyone *asks for this recipe, yet the ingredients are perfectly everyday and the method simple. It is wonderful served hot with jacket potatoes, grilled tomatoes, mushrooms and Brussels sprouts, or cold as a picnic main course with a crisp green salad and a robust home-made coleslaw.*

Serves 4

2 oz (50 g) butter

1 lb (450 g) onions, peeled and finely chopped

2 fat cloves garlic, peeled and crushed (optional)

2 teaspoons Marmite

8 oz (225 g) porridge oats

6–8 oz (175–225 g) Cheddar cheese, grated

1–2 tablespoons finely chopped mixed fresh herbs or 2–3 teaspoons mixed dried herbs

2 large eggs, lightly beaten

Pinch of salt

Freshly ground black pepper

Pre-heat the oven to gas mark 5, 375°F (190°C).

In a very large heavy frying-pan melt the butter and gently fry the onions and garlic (if using), stirring them around occasionally, until they are soft and transparent, but do not allow them to brown. Stir in the Marmite and allow it to melt into the onions. Now tip the onions into a large mixing bowl and stir in the porridge oats, grated cheese and herbs, mixing well with a large spoon. Add the eggs and season the mixture to taste with salt and pepper. The mixture should be stiffish and of a dropping consistency.

Turn into a lightly buttered 8–9 inch (20–23 cm) baking dish or deep flan dish and bake in the oven for about 40 minutes or until firm and golden-brown on top. To serve, slice into wedges at the table.

Gougère of creamy young vegetables

A light, savoury and delicate main course for which you can choose young tender parsnips, turnips, Jerusalem artichokes or kohlrabi: they have similar yet distinctive tastes. I particularly like this dish made with kohlrabi, a much underrated vegetable. Serve with potatoes and a salad of watercress and lettuce.

Serves 4

10 oz (275 g) young parsnips, turnips, Jerusalem artichokes or kohlrabi, peeled and finely diced

Pinch of salt

Freshly ground white pepper

1 oz (25 g) butter plus extra for greasing

1 small onion, peeled and very finely chopped

1 oz (25 g) flour

10 fl oz (300 ml) milk

1 teaspoon fresh or ½ teaspoon dried marjoram

2 oz (50 g) Cheddar cheese, finely grated

2 oz (50 g) breadcrumbs, toasted

Finely chopped parsley to garnish

Choux Paste:

2 oz (50 g) butter

5 fl oz (150 ml) water

2½ oz (65 g) flour, sifted

A little white pepper

½ teaspoon mustard powder

About 2 eggs, lightly beaten

2 oz (50 g) Cheddar cheese, grated

First lightly season the prepared vegetable with salt and pepper and steam until very tender. Set aside. Meanwhile, melt the butter in a saucepan and gently fry the onion until it is soft but not brown. Add the flour, stir and cook through for a minute. Gradually add the milk, stirring all the time to make a smooth sauce, and add the marjoram. Continue cooking gently, stirring constantly, for about 5 minutes. Add the cooked vegetable – you should have a fairly bulky mixture in the delicately flavoured sauce. Set aside.

Prepare the choux paste. Bring the butter and water to the boil in a saucepan. Because you are going to add the flour, pepper and mustard powder to the pan very quickly, have it ready on a sheet of paper with a fold to make a chute. When the butter and water boil, turn off the heat and shoot in the flour mixture in one go. Beat madly with a wooden spoon until the paste leaves the side of the pan. Let it cool a little, then beat in the eggs and cheese until you have a smooth and glossy paste: you may need slightly less or more than 2 eggs, but you must not let the paste become too wet.

When you are ready to cook, pre-heat the oven to gas mark 6, 400°F (200°C).

Lightly butter a large flan dish or baking sheet and put two thirds of the paste into/on to it. Remembering that the paste is going to swell and puff up to double its size, spread it out and dip your fingers in warm water to hollow out the centre. Fill with the vegetable mixture. Using a dessertspoon, partly cover the filling with little balls of the remaining paste, making a circle of them inside the rim of the base. Scatter the centre with the grated cheese and breadcrumbs. Bake for approximately 25–30 minutes or until golden and puffed up. Dust with the chopped parsley and serve immediately.

Joffy's pilaff

I created this for one of my sons who is very tall and healthy in spite of his diet of mashed potatoes with 'things' or rice with 'other things'. The basic process of cooking a pilaff is very adaptable: the spices and nuts can be replaced by other ingredients, or a plainer pilaff can be prepared to serve with other dishes. Kidney, soya or mung beans can be used in place of the chickpeas if you wish.

Serves 4

3–4 tablespoons olive oil

2 medium onions, peeled and finely chopped

2 fat cloves garlic, peeled and finely chopped

½ teaspoon chilli powder

1 teaspoon ground ginger

1 teaspoon ground coriander

Freshly ground black pepper

8 oz (225 g) almonds, blanched and split

2 oz (50 g) pine nuts

2 oz (50 g) sultanas or raisins

5 oz (150 g) natural yoghurt

8 oz (225 g) basmati rice

About 15 fl oz (400 ml) vegetable stock

6 oz (175 g) fresh peas (shelled weight) or frozen peas

4 oz (110 g) tinned chickpeas or dried chickpeas, soaked in water for 24 hours and boiled for at least 2 hours

Chopped hard-boiled eggs and chopped fresh coriander to garnish

Heat the oil in a large heavy-bottomed pan. Gently fry the onions and garlic until they are soft but not brown. Add the spices and pepper and stir. Now add the almonds and pine nuts and continue cooking until they are golden. Stir in the sultanas or raisins and the yoghurt and bring to simmering point. Stir in the rice and cook for a minute or so until the rice is well coated, then add the vegetable stock, which should just cover the rice by ¼ inch (5 mm). Stir in the green peas and chickpeas. Cover the pan tightly and cook over a low heat without even peeping for 20 minutes. Tip into a large warmed serving dish and garnish with chopped hard-boiled eggs and chopped fresh coriander leaves. Hand more natural yoghurt separately if you wish.

Fried rice with Brussels sprouts, eggs and nuts

This crunchy green stir-fry is a versatile way of producing a quick nutritious supper: chopped spring greens, Chinese leaves or broccoli can be substituted for the sprouts. The sesame-seed seasoning is available from oriental food shops.

Serves 4

2 tablespoons sunflower or sesame oil

2 large eggs, lightly beaten

1 lb (450 g) cooked brown rice

8 oz (225 g) small Brussels sprouts, trimmed and quartered

2 sticks celery, sliced finely

1 fresh red chilli, de-seeded and finely chopped

4 oz (110 g) button mushrooms, thinly sliced

1–2 tablespoons light soy sauce

1–2 teaspoons brown sugar

1 bunch spring onions, trimmed and sliced on the diagonal, including the good green parts

4–6 oz (110–175 g) cashew or pine nuts, toasted if liked

Freshly ground black pepper

White and black sesame-seed seasoning

Make sure that all your ingredients are prepared and assembled before you begin to cook. Have ready a large warmed serving dish and 4 warmed plates.

Heat a large wok or frying-pan, add 1 tablespoon of the oil and swirl it around. As soon as you can detect a slight haze, throw in the eggs and tilt the pan to form a large omelette. As it reaches setting point, add the rice and use a spatula to break up the omelette. Mix well and stir-fry for 2 minutes until heated through. Transfer to the warmed dish.

Now give the wok or frying-pan a quick wipe with kitchen paper, return it to the heat and add the remaining 1 tablespoon oil. Add the sprouts, celery and chilli and stir-fry for 1 minute. Keep everything moving! Add the mushrooms and stir-fry for 30 seconds. Turn the heat down a little, add the soy sauce and brown sugar and cook gently for 1 minute. Tip in the rice and egg, add the spring onions, nuts and pepper to taste and cook, stirring all the time, for a final minute until all is heated through. Tip back into the serving dish, sprinkle with the sesame-seed seasoning and serve immediately.

Sauces

Herb oil

Take a bunch of fresh herbs of your choice, put them in a clean jam jar and then fill up the jar with a light oil such as safflower (olive oil already has a strong distinctive flavour). Cover the jar and leave it in a warm place for about 3 weeks. Then remove the herbs (which will have become blackish) and strain carefully through kitchen or coffee filter paper. The oil will now have a lovely green colour and can be stored in a bottle in the refrigerator for several months. Use to enhance all kinds of barbecued meats.

Hot mango and coriander dipping sauce

3 tablespoons mango chutney

2–3 tablespoons lemon or lime juice

8 oz (225 g) fromage frais

2 tablespoons mayonnaise

2 tablespoons Greek yoghurt

1 teaspoon curry powder

2 tablespoons finely chopped fresh coriander

Gently whisk all the ingredients together, then chill for 1–2 hours to make a superbly arresting barbecue dip.

Fresh tomato sauce

1–1½ lb (500–750 g) ripe, juicy tomatoes, peeled and de-seeded

1 tablespoon olive oil

½ tablespoon finely chopped fresh herbs

1–2 teaspoons tomato purée

Freshly ground black pepper

Place all the ingredients in a large heavy pan and simmer for 15 minutes, stirring occasionally, until the sauce is reduced. If the colour is pale, add a little more tomato purée. Serve the sauce hot or cold. You can process it in a food processor or blender if you want a smoother texture.

Alternative mayonnaise

For those who are concerned about the risk factor in using raw egg yolks in conventional mayonnaise, it is now possible to buy pasteurised eggs from leading supermarkets and food halls. Alternatively, here is Mrs Beeton's recipe for a 'cooked' mayonnaise:

1 tablespoon salad oil

1 tablespoon sugar

1 teaspoon salt

1 dessertspoon mustard

3 egg yolks, lightly beaten

10 fl oz (300 ml) milk or single cream

5 fl oz (150 ml) white wine vinegar

Mix the oil, sugar, salt and mustard together in a basin. Add the lightly beaten egg yolks, then the milk or cream and then the vinegar. Put the mixture in a double boiler or in a basin set over a pan of simmering water and cook, stirring constantly, until a thick creamy consistency is achieved. Do not allow the mixture to boil. Cool and refrigerate until needed.

Aïoli

6 cloves garlic (or to taste)

Pinch of salt

2 egg yolks

10 fl oz (300 ml) good-quality olive oil

Squeeze of lemon juice

Freshly ground black pepper

Pound the garlic with a pinch of salt until thoroughly mashed – use a pestle and mortar, or the end of a wooden rolling pin or back of a wooden spoon in a sturdy bowl. Add the egg yolks and beat with a wooden spoon. Now add the oil drop by drop, beating all the time, and continue until the sauce thickens and all the oil is incorporated. When the mixture is smooth and creamy, beat in a little fresh lemon juice and freshly ground black pepper to taste.

Two simple dipping sauces

Both these sauces are very good for dunking skewers of rare beef in, or sizzling morsels of fish or shellfish. The horseradish powder used in Sauce 2 is obtainable from oriental food shops.

Sauce 1:

1 inch (2.5 cm) cube fresh root ginger

3 tablespoons light soy sauce

Peel and grate the ginger (you should have about 1 tablespoon) and mix well with the soy sauce.

Sauce 2:

1 tablespoon horseradish powder

4 tablespoons dark soy sauce

Simply mix the ingredients thoroughly together.

Cool yoghurt and mint sauce

1 clove garlic, peeled and crushed with a little salt

Pinch of sea salt

1 bunch spring onions, trimmed and finely sliced, including all the good green parts

1 handful finely chopped fresh mint (or to taste)

About 5 fl oz (150 ml) natural yoghurt

Combine all the ingredients and chill for at least 4 hours before serving with lamb.

A spicy pepper relish

6 cloves garlic, peeled and finely sliced

1 bunch spring onions, trimmed and sliced, including all the good green parts

2–3 green peppers, de-seeded and chopped

2–3 fresh green chillies, de-seeded and chopped

3 tablespoons good-quality olive oil

Pinch of salt

Plenty of freshly ground black pepper

Cook all the ingredients slowly in the olive oil in a heavy pan over a gentle heat for about 10 minutes or until they are soft. Cool and store in the refrigerator; the hot hotness gradually diminishes after a few days! This is good with steaks or chops and pitta bread.

Béchamel sauce

2 oz (50 g) butter

2 oz (50 g) white or wholemeal flour

1 pt (570 ml) skimmed or semi-skimmed milk

1 blade mace (optional)

1 bay leaf

1 shallot, very finely chopped

Pinch of salt, freshly ground black pepper

Melt the butter in a heavy saucepan, stir in the flour and cook for 2 minutes on a very low heat. This stage is very important because if the flour is not thoroughly cooked, the sauce will have a strong floury flavour.

Slide the pan off the heat and whisk in a little milk with a balloon whisk. Add the rest of the milk a little at a time, whisking constantly so that there are no lumps. Now return the sauce to the heat, add the mace (if using), bay leaf and finely chopped shallot, bring up to just under simmering point and cook for 10 minutes, stirring all the time. Season to taste and remove the bay leaf.

Further reading and useful addresses

British Food Finds, an annual directory of fine British foods, edited by Henrietta Green, and published by Rich and Green: contains a selective regional list of quality producers of meat, game, poultry, fish, cheese, horticultural produce, cereals and grains, preserves and drinks.

Food from Britain are compiling a comprehensive guide to producers, with an emphasis on speciality foods and quality. Information may be obtained from Food from Britain, 301–344 Market Towers, New Covent Garden, London SW8 5NQ, telephone: 01 720 2144.

The Soil Association, 86 Colston Street, Bristol BS1 5BB, telephone 0272 290661. Aims to promote organic food and farming, and can supply a complete national list of organic growers and farmers that have the Soil Association Symbol. They also have regional lists of the same, usually covering 5 counties. They also publish a *Meat List* which is a complete nationwide guide to farms, butchers and retailers of organically raised meat with Soil Association Symbol.

The Game Conservancy, Fordingbridge, Hampshire SP6 1EF, telephone 0425 52381, have leaflets and information on game and wildlife conservation.

National Game Dealers' Association, 1 Belgrove, Tunbridge Wells, Kent TN1 1YW, telephone 0892 541412, can supply a list of licensed game dealers.

Compassion in World Farming, 20 Lavant Street, Petersfield, Hampshire GU32 3EW, telephone 0730 64208, and their educational wing The Athene Trust, is the leading group campaigning for an end to factory farming and a fair deal for all farm animals. Educational booklets and videos are available.

Farm Shop and Pick Your Own Association, write to Jane Connor, The Secretary of the association at Agriculture House, Knightsbridge, London SW1X 7NJ, telephone 01 235 5077.

Heal Farm Quality Traditional Meats (Anne Petch), Kings Nympton, Umberleigh, Devon EX37 9TB, telephone 07695 2077, member of Rare Breeds Survival Trust and Approved Centre – traditional breeds of pork, beef, lamb, venison available by mail order – all animals reared in a nonintensive system without the aid of growth-promoters etc.

The Real Meat Company Limited, East Hill Farm, Heytesbury, Warminster, Wiltshire BA12 0HR, telephone 0985 40436/40060, has a wide range of quality meats and poultry raised following the company's welfare code which is based on the mandates of Compassion in World Farming, the aims of the RSPCA and on the Ministry of Agriculture's own very good, but unenforced code. Available at their own retail outlets in London and Bath and by mail order.

I am still trying to find a list of compassionate butchers – but this may be covered by Soil Association list.

Books:

The Green Consumer Guide, John Elkington and Julia Hailes (Victor Gollancz 1988).
The New Organic Food Guide, Allan Gear, contains inspirational chapters on food and farming, and a large number of useful addresses of suppliers etc. (Dent 1987).
On Food and Cooking, Harold McGee (Unwin Hyman 1988).
Classic Game Cookery, compiled for the Game Conservancy by Julia Drysdale (Papermac 1983), available from bookshops and by mail order from the Game Conservancy (see above for address).
Game for All, Nichola Fletcher (Victor Gollancz 1987).
Mastering the Art of French Cooking, Simone Beck (Penguin 1978).
The Cooking of South West France, Paula Wolfert (Dorling Kindersley 1988).
Jane Grigson's Vegetable Book (Penguin 1980) and *The Observer Guide to British Cookery* (Michael Joseph 1984).
Spices, Salt and Aromatics in the English Kitchen (Penguin 1970) and *French Provincial Cooking* (Penguin 1964), both by Elizabeth David.
Food for Free, by Richard Mabey, a guide to the edible wild plants of Britain (Fontana 1975).
Cooking with Sea Vegetables, Peter and Montse Bradford (Thorsons 1985).
Wild Food, Roger Phillips (Pan 1983) – a unique photographic guide to finding, cooking and eating wild plants, mushrooms and seaweed.
Scarista Style: A Free-Range and Humane Approach to Cooking and Eating, Alison Johnson (Victor Gollancz 1987).

Index